The
MOST INSPIRING
HOCKEY STORIES
OF ALL TIME
FOR YOUNG CANADIANS
(COLORED INTERIOR & PHOTOS)
2024
Dr. Fanatomy

Bonus Booklet For You!

With great pleasure, I warmly welcome you to purchase the book. Congratulations on stepping towards improving yourself and developing the skills necessary to thrive as a teenager and beyond.

Below is a surprise gift for you!

Download it from the link (or scan the QR code below) – https://bit.ly/TeeNavigationBonus

TABLE OF CONTENTS

TABLE OF CONTENTS

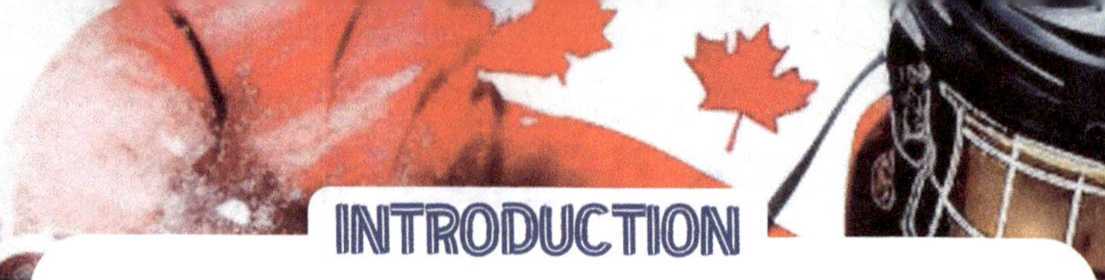

INTRODUCTION

Stories from the Heart of the Rink

Welcome, my young friend! Take a seat, and let's delve into the heart of Canada's beloved pastime - hockey. This journey contains incredible stories, and I am here to share them with you. Imagine you and I sitting by a warm crackling fire, sipping on hot cocoa, while I narrate these tales.

Hockey is not just a sport in Canada; it is a passion that runs deep in the nation's veins. From the moment the first puck hits the ice in those frozen ponds and backyard rinks to the roaring cheers in packed arenas, Canadians carry the love of the game with them wherever they go.

What makes this sport truly magical are the legends, heroes, and dreamers who have graced the ice, each leaving an indelible mark on the game. They are not just players, from Wayne Gretzky's dazzling skills to Bobby Orr's elegance on the blue line and Maurice "Rocket" Richard's sheer scoring prowess. They are our inspirations, the ones who've shown us that we can reach for the stars with unwavering dedication.

This book is a treasure chest of inspiring stories about hockey players. It celebrates their resilience, determination, and Canadian spirit. As you read, you will delve into the very essence of the sport: the frozen ponds, the companionship of teammates, and the cherished traditions that bring us together.

You will learn about the game's values, the unspoken code of sportsmanship, and the invaluable lessons that hockey teaches us all.

Also, we would meet the amazing women who've broken hockey barriers - Hayley Wickenheiser and Marie-Philip Poulin. Discover young heroes who dared to dream, laced up their skates, and carry the torch forward.

Our journey continues with the exploration of on-ice contributors. We will also delve into the world behind the scenes, including the role of coaches, mentors, and officials. Through this, you will understand that hockey is a team effort, both on and off the ice.

In addition, we will talk to young players like you to give you a glimpse of the future. They will share their dreams, passions, and words of wisdom they have gathered throughout their journeys.

Dear young hockey enthusiast, I warmly welcome you to turn the page and immerse yourself in the stories that have shaped Canadian hockey. These tales have the power to ignite and fuel your dreams. They serve as a reminder that with passion, commitment, and a genuine love for the game, you too can be a part of this magical world of hockey.

1. LEGENDS OF THE ICE

- Wayne Gretzky: The Great One
- Bobby Orr: A Defenseman's Dream
- Maurice "Rocket" Richard: Scoring Sensation

WAYNE GRETZKY: THE GREAT ONE

Attribution: By Hakandahlstrom (Håkan Dahlström). IrisKawling uploaded later versions at en. wikipedia. - Originally from en. Wikipedia; description page is/was here. Can also be found at Flickr. CC BY-SA 3.0. https://commons.wikimedia.org/w/index.php?curid=3545164

Let me tell you a story about a young Canadian boy who became the greatest hockey player ever. His name is Wayne Gretzky, and he's known as "The Great One." Gather around and listen closely to his tale.

Wayne was born in Brantford, Ontario, a town like many others nationwide. However, what set him apart was his exceptional talent for playing hockey. He could perform impressive feats with a hockey puck that left everyone in awe. He could shoot a puck into a washing machine from 20 feet away as a child, demonstrating his exceptional skills.

Wayne's rise to greatness was not solely due to his natural talent but also his hard work and unwavering love for the game. He devoted countless hours to practicing, honing his shots, and mastering the sport's subtleties. His determination and passion for hockey were boundless.

Wayne's exceptional skills on the ice drew attention as he grew older. At the remarkable age of 17, he made his debut in the National Hockey League (NHL). Most players his age would only occasionally get a chance to play in the NHL, but Wayne was different. He was not just another player; he was a game-changer.

During his career, Wayne Gretzky set records that still stand today. He is the all-time leading scorer in the history of the NHL, with an astounding 2,857 points to his name. This is more points than any other player in the league's history has scored. Just imagine that, young one! Gretzky's career included an unbelievable 61 records, including the most points in a single season (215) and the most goals in a single season (92). These are records that only the greatest can achieve.

Wayne's exceptional ability to read the game made him even more special. He had the remarkable skill of anticipating plays and moves before they happened, almost like he could see into the future. Wayne was a true team player who always put the team first, and his exceptional skills, sportsmanship, and team-first attitude earned him the captain's "C" for his teams. He set an example for his teammates, demonstrating the importance of playing with integrity and putting the team's success above personal achievements.

What can we learn from Wayne Gretzky's story, my young friend? We can see that talent is only the beginning. Hard work, dedication, and an unyielding passion for the game can make all the difference. Wayne's journey from the Brantford rinks to the grand NHL arenas is an inspiring example of what a young puck enthusiast can achieve with perseverance and an unwavering love for the sport.

But this is just the beginning of our exploration into the world of Canadian hockey legends. We have more incredible stories to discover, tales of dedication, triumph, and unforgettable moments that continue to inspire the next generation of Canadian hockey players. So, let's keep going, shall we?

BOBBY ORR: A DEFENSEMAN'S DREAM

Attribution: By Aaron Frutman - Flickr: The great Bobby Orr loving it, CC BY 2.0, https://commons.wikimedia.org/w/index.php?curid=24296012

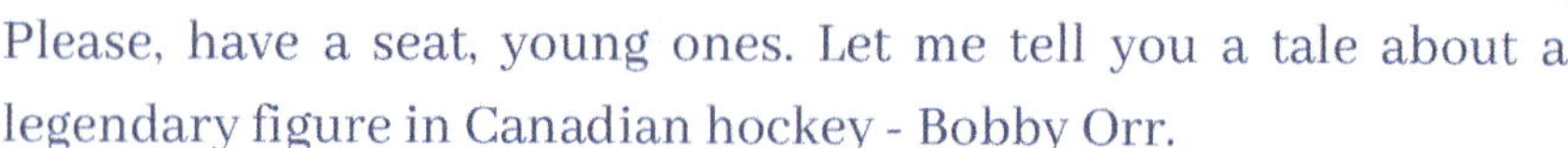

Please, have a seat, young ones. Let me tell you a tale about a legendary figure in Canadian hockey - Bobby Orr.

Bobby Orr was not just a hockey player; he was a defenseman. Hailing from Parry Sound, Ontario, a small town like many across our great country, he stood out like a shining star on the ice.

Bobby's passion for hockey started at a young age when he would put on his skates and head to the frozen ponds of Parry Sound to hone his skating and puck-handling skills. There's something magical about those frozen ponds that inspire young players like Bobby to pursue their dreams.

As he grew older, Bobby's talent as a defenseman became apparent. He had a unique ability to control the game from the blue line, effectively defending his team's goal while also contributing to the offense by setting up and scoring goals. Bobby's style of play redefined what it meant to be a defenseman in hockey.

Bobby Orr's National Hockey League (NHL) career was magnificent. He won eight consecutive Norris Trophies for being the best defenseman, which is still an unbeaten record. However, it wasn't just about the awards and recognition but about his unique style and enthusiasm for the game that set him apart.

One of hockey's most memorable moments occurred in 1970 during the Stanley Cup Final, where Bobby Orr's Boston Bruins played against the St. Louis Blues. It was an overtime game, and as Bobby scored the winning goal, he was captured flying through the air, his arms outstretched in celebration.

  That iconic image is ingrained in the minds of hockey fans worldwide. It was more than just a goal; it symbolized Bobby's zeal and impact on the game.

The story of my young friend Bobby Orr is unique because he proved that there are no limits to what one can achieve. As a defenseman, he became the best in the world, and his style of play transformed how the game was played. His journey from the frozen ponds in Parry Sound to the grand arenas of the NHL is a testament to the power of passion and a relentless pursuit of excellence.

And this is just the beginning of our journey into the world of Canadian hockey legends. We will uncover more incredible stories of dedication, triumph, and unforgettable moments that continue to inspire the next generation of Canadian hockey players. So, are you ready for the next story, my young puck enthusiast?

MAURICE "ROCKET" RICHARD: SCORING SENSATION

Attribution: By Conrad Poirier - File:Hockey. Maurice Richard BAnQ P48S1P12157.jpg. Public Domain, https://commons.wikimedia.org/w/index.php?curid=37797587

Allow me to tell you a story about a legendary hockey player named Maurice Richard, also known as "The Rocket". He was a remarkable scorer whose story began in Montreal, Quebec. Just like you, he was once a young, passionate kid who loved hockey. Born on August 4, 1921, he grew up in a world that was vastly different from what we know today, but his love for hockey remained just as strong.

Maurice, also known as "The Rocket", was a dominant force on the ice. He played for the Montreal Canadiens, a team that has always been a symbol of pride for Canadians. But what made Maurice exceptional was his remarkable ability to score goals.

Despite not being the biggest or fastest player, Maurice possessed an unmatched skill with the puck and an unyielding determination. His agility and powerful shot made him a scoring machine. In fact, he became the first player in the history of the National Hockey League (NHL) to score 50 goals in 50 games, a record that remains one of the greatest achievements in the sport's history.

Maurice Richard was not only a great player but also an emblem of hope and inspiration for many. In the 1940s and 50s, hockey was more than just a game in Canada; it was a part of their culture. People from all walks of life looked up to Maurice, and he became a symbol of determination and success. He proved that even the most minor player on the ice could achieve greatness with hard work and unwavering dedication.

Furthermore, Maurice Richard was a hero off the ice too. In 1955, a significant event took place.

Maurice was suspended during a game, which made the fans in Montreal unhappy. However, they remarkably supported him by starting a protest that went down in history as the "Richard Riot." It was a moment when people stood up for their beliefs, significantly impacting the sport and society.

What can we learn from Maurice "The Rocket" Richard? We can learn that no matter how big or small you are and regardless of where you come from, with passion and determination, you can achieve greatness. Maurice's story is a testament to the power of believing in yourself and standing up for what you believe is right.

Furthermore, this is just the beginning of our journey into the world of Canadian hockey legends. We'll uncover more incredible stories of dedication, triumph, and unforgettable moments that continue to inspire the next generation of Canadian hockey players. Are you ready for the next story, my young puck enthusiast?

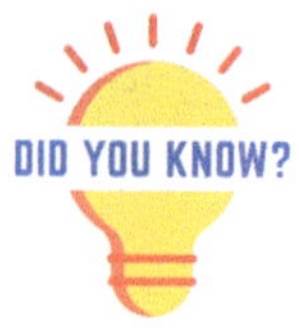

- Wayne Gretzky, known as "The Great One," holds over 60 NHL records. One of his most remarkable records is scoring 50 goals in just 39 games.

- In 1970, Bobby Orr scored a legendary goal that clinched the Stanley Cup for the Boston Bruins. The iconic image of him flying through the air, celebrating the goal, is one of the most famous in sports history.

- Maurice "Rocket" Richard was given his nickname due to his incredible speed on the ice. He was the first player in NHL history to score 50 goals in one season.

- Wayne Gretzky became the Edmonton Oilers' captain at 22, making him the youngest captain in NHL history.

- Bobby Orr won the Norris Trophy as the NHL's best defenseman for eight consecutive years, a still-standing record.

- Maurice Richard was the first player in NHL history to score a hat trick (three goals in one game) in all three games of a playoff series.

- Wayne Gretzky holds the record for the longest point streak in NHL history, with an astounding 51 consecutive games with at least one point.

- In the 1970-71 season, Bobby Orr became the first defenseman to lead the NHL in playoff scoring and win the Hart Trophy as the league's Most Valuable Player in the same year.

- Maurice Richard's suspension in 1955 led to the infamous "Richard Riot" in Montreal, where fans protested his suspension, making it a historic moment in hockey history.

- Wayne Gretzky holds the record for the most assists in an NHL career with a staggering 1,963 assists, showcasing his incredible playmaking ability.

2. STANLEY CUP GLORY

- The Quest for Lord Stanley's Cup
- Historic Stanley Cup Moments
- Canadian Dominance in the NHL

THE QUEST FOR LORD STANLEY'S CUP

I want to share a story from the Stanley Cup Finals that depicts determination, resilience, and the remarkable bond between a player and his team. In the spring of 1971, the Montreal Canadiens competed against the Chicago Black Hawks in the finals. The series was intense, and each game was a fierce battle on the ice. The two teams were evenly matched, and the outcome of the pivotal Game 7 would determine the championship winner.

In the series' final game, the Canadiens had to play without their captain, Jean Béliveau, who was one of their star players but was sidelined due to an injury. The stakes were high, and the atmosphere in the Montreal Forum was charged with excitement. With the score tied at 2-2 in the third period, the Canadiens' head coach, Al MacNeil, made a bold move. He sent out Henri Richard, a player known as the "Pocket Rocket" because of his smaller stature, to take Béliveau's place on the ice.

Henri Richard, the younger brother of Maurice "The Rocket" Richard, may not have been a prolific goal scorer like his famous sibling, but he had an unwavering determination to win that was second to none. He personified the spirit of the Canadiens. As the clock ticked down and the tension in the arena mounted, Henri Richard found himself in the perfect position and scored the winning goal, leading the Montreal Canadiens to victory and securing the Stanley Cup.

The atmosphere was electric as the crowd erupted into cheers. The players lifted the Cup, celebrating with Henri Richard amid the jubilation.

This moment was a perfect example of the depth of the Canadiens' team spirit and their ability to overcome any adversity.

Henri Richard's story is a testament that heroes come in all sizes. It's not about the number of goals you score but the heart you put into the game. It's about stepping up when your team needs you the most and seizing the moment.

The night the players celebrated with the Stanley Cup was remarkable as they had come together as a team, faced adversity, and emerged as champions. This moment united the city of Montreal and the entire nation in celebration.

It's important to remember that the Stanley Cup is not just about the big stars; it's about a team's collective spirit and heart and the enduring love for the game. Stories like Henri Richard's continue to inspire us and remind us that in hockey, as in life, it's not the player's size but the size of the heart that matters.There are many incredible stories from the world of Canadian hockey legends, and as our journey continues, we'll uncover more tales of dedication, triumph, and unforgettable moments. Are you ready for the next chapter in our adventure, my young puck enthusiast?

HISTORIC STANLEY CUP MOMENTS

The story is about a memorable event that left a lasting mark on the history of the Stanley Cup.

In 1952, the Detroit Red Wings faced the Montreal Canadiens in the Stanley Cup Finals. The series was tied at 3-3, and it all came down to the thrilling Game 7.

The game was a fiercely contested battle, with both teams giving it their all. The tension in the arena was palpable. The Canadiens had a goalie named Gerry McNeil, who was playing instead of their injured star Jacques Plante. McNeil had the game of his life, making save after save to keep his team in the match.

The game was tied 3-3 as the clock wound down, and it looked like the result could be decided in overtime. Suddenly, with only 1:22 left on the clock, Maurice "The Rocket" Richard of the Canadiens received a pass from his teammate Bernie "Boom Boom" Geoffrion.

Maurice Richard was known for his scoring ability and for stepping up when it mattered most. With sheer determination, he made a move that left everyone in awe. He deked around the Red Wings' defense and, in one swift motion, fired the puck into the net.

The crowd in the Montreal Forum erupted in joy, and the Canadiens took the lead with just over a minute remaining. The Red Wings fought desperately to equalize, but Gerry McNeil's stellar goaltending held them off.When the final buzzer sounded, the Canadiens had won the game 4-3 and captured the Stanley Cup.

It was not just any Cup victory, but a moment that etched its place in history.

Maurice Richard's game-winning goal in the dying moments of Game 7 has become one of the most iconic moments in Stanley Cup history. It was a testament to his skill, determination, and ability to perform under pressure.

The Montreal Forum was filled with cheers and celebrations as Maurice Richard brought the Cup to Montreal once again. This Stanley Cup moment reminds us that magic can happen in a blink of an eye in hockey. It's about unforgettable moments that remind us why the Stanley Cup is not just a trophy but a symbol of our deepest hockey dreams.

Remember this story as you watch the Stanley Cup games, for in every game, there's the potential for history to be made, for heroes to rise, and for dreams to come true. Our journey continues with more stories of dedication, triumph, and unforgettable moments that will inspire the next generation of Canadian hockey players. Ready for the next story in our adventure? Let's go!

CANADIAN DOMINANCE IN THE NHL

Dear friend, I would like to share a fascinating story about the time when Canadian teams dominated the National Hockey League (NHL).

Let's travel back to the 1980s, a time when Canadian hockey was at its peak. During this era, Canadian teams ruled the NHL, and it seemed like the Stanley Cup would always end up in the Great White North.

During the 1980s, Canadian hockey fans were captivated by a fierce rivalry between two teams from Alberta - the Edmonton Oilers and the Calgary Flames. Both teams were incredibly talented and driven to win.

In 1983, the Edmonton Oilers, led by their young superstar Wayne Gretzky, made it to the Stanley Cup Finals, where they faced off against the New York Islanders. Despite their best efforts, they fell short of winning the Cup. However, this was just the beginning of their journey towards future success.

In 1984, the Oilers made it to the Finals once again and this time, they won the Stanley Cup, bringing immense joy to Edmonton and Canada. The Oilers were invincible, and Wayne Gretzky was at the peak of his career.

The following year, in 1985, the Oilers reclaimed the Cup, and Gretzky continued breaking records and inspiring a new generation of Canadian players. It was a time when young hockey enthusiasts across the country dreamed of becoming the next Gretzky.

Canadian dominance continued with the Calgary Flames, who were led by their captain, Lanny McDonald, and reached the Stanley Cup Finals in 1986. Although they missed winning the Cup, their journey was a source of inspiration for fans in Calgary and across Canada.

In 1987, it was the Oilers' turn once again, and they secured the Cup. By this time, Wayne Gretzky had become a household name, not only in Canada but around the world. He was a symbol of Canadian excellence on the ice.

The 1980s were an era of Canadian hockey dominance in the NHL. Canadian teams and players were celebrated and admired, not only for their skill but for the passion and heart they brought to the game.

This story reminds us that Canadian hockey has a rich history of success that inspires young players to dream big and aim for the highest levels of the sport. It's a testament to Canadians' enduring love and dedication to the game of hockey.

So, as you watch today's NHL games, remember the era when Canadian teams shone bright, and let it inspire you to chase your own hockey dreams. The legacy of those times lives on, and countless stories are waiting to be written by the next generation of Canadian hockey stars.

This is just one of the many incredible stories from the world of Canadian hockey legends. Our journey continues with more tales of dedication, triumph, and unforgettable moments that will inspire the next generation of Canadian hockey players.

Trivia Fact	Description
Origins of the Cup	Donated by Lord Stanley in 1892 as a challenge cup for the best amateur hockey team in Canada.
Oldest Professional Trophy	The oldest professional sports trophy in North America, with a history dating back to the 19th century.
Montreal Canadiens' Dominance	The Montreal Canadiens have won the most Stanley Cups in history, with 24 championships as of 2021.
Original Composition	The original Stanley Cup was much smaller than the modern version, standing just 7.28 inches tall.
Three-Part Trophy	The Stanley Cup consists of three parts: the cup itself, the collar, and the base, each with its own history and engravings.
Secret Inscriptions	Names of winning players, coaches, and staff are engraved on the Cup's bands, with the location of names for each year kept secret.
Traveling Trophy	The Cup has traveled worldwide, visiting war zones, mountain tops, and even the bottom of swimming pools with winning teams.
24/7 Guardian	The Cup has a designated guardian known as the "Keeper of the Cup" who ensures its safety and accompanies it on its journeys.
Stolen and Recovered	In 1970, the Cup was stolen from the Hockey Hall of Fame in Toronto but was later found in a snowbank.
Multiple Versions	There are multiple Stanley Cups in existence, with the original displayed in the Hockey Hall of Fame and a new Cup created each year for the winning team.

3. THE HEROES' JOURNEYS

- Kid Heroes of the NHL
- Rookie Sensations
- Young Players Who Captured Hearts

KID HEROES OF THE NHL

Once upon a time, in the small town of Cole Harbour, Nova Scotia, a young boy named Sidney Crosby put on his skates and took his first strides onto the icy wonderland of a local pond. At the time, no one could have predicted that this young boy, with dreams as vast as the frozen horizon, would one day become a hockey legend and a hero to young hockey enthusiasts across Canada.

Sidney's love for hockey started when he was just a kid. His father built a small rink in their backyard, and Sidney spent countless hours practicing, honing his skills, and dreaming of one day making it to the big leagues.As the years passed, Sidney's passion and talent for the game grew stronger with each season. He played with a fire in his heart and a determination to be the best. Even at a young age, he exhibited maturity and a work ethic that set him apart from his peers.

Sidney Crosby achieved a remarkable feat at 16 when he became the youngest player in the history of the Quebec Major Junior Hockey League (QMJHL) to score 100 points in a single season. His exceptional skills often drew comparisons to the greatest players in NHL history.

However, Sidney's true greatness lay not only in his abilities but also in his humility, love for the game, and values. He believed that to be a hero, one must be more than just a skilled player.

In 2005, Sidney was drafted first overall by the Pittsburgh Penguins in the NHL at 18. Despite immense pressure, he rose to the occasion and became one of the league's brightest stars, both on and off the ice, serving as a role model for others.

In 2009, Sidney Crosby and the Pittsburgh Penguins won the Stanley Cup, marking a moment of triumph not only for the team but also for a young kid from Cole Harbour who had captivated the hearts of Canadians. Sidney Crosby's journey from a small town to the NHL inspired young players nationwide, demonstrating that hard work, dedication, and a love for the game can make dreams come true.

So, as you watch your favorite hockey players on TV, remember that they too were once kids with big dreams like you. The story of Sidney Crosby is a reminder that heroes can come from unexpected places, and sometimes, they start as kids with a passion for the game.

And this is just one of the many incredible stories of Kid Heroes in the NHL. Our journey continues with more tales of young players who have captured the hearts of hockey fans across Canada.

By Michael Miller - Own work, CC BY-SA 4.0, https://commons.wikimedia.org/w/index.php?curid=76195294

ROOKIE SENSATIONS

Once upon a time, in a rink not far from the heart of Toronto, there was a young rookie named Auston Matthews. Auston had a dream of playing in the National Hockey League (NHL) and making a name for himself. Little did he know that he was about to embark on a journey that would capture the hearts of hockey fans across Canada.

Auston Matthews grew up in Scottsdale, Arizona, a place not exactly known as a hockey hotbed. Nevertheless, his passion for the game burned brighter than the desert sun. He practiced and played day in and day out, with his sights firmly set on the NHL.

Auston's dream came true in 2016 when he was selected first overall by the Toronto Maple Leafs in the NHL Draft at just 19 years old, making him the youngest player ever to be drafted first overall. As a rookie, he faced pressure as Toronto, a city that lives and breathes hockey, was counting on him to make a difference. However, Auston didn't disappoint. In his NHL debut, he scored an incredible feat of four goals, which no other player had achieved in their debut.

Auston's rookie season was nothing short of magical. He displayed impressive skills, speed, and a knack for scoring that left fans in awe. He broke records and set new ones, becoming the first rookie to score 40 goals for the Maple Leafs in over a century.

What made Auston Matthews a true sensation was not just his talent, but his love for the game. He played with a smile on his face, making fans believe anything was possible.

In recognition of his outstanding performance, Auston Matthews was named the Calder Trophy winner in 2016, an award given to the league's top rookie. He captured the hearts of Maple Leafs fans and inspired young players across Canada.

Auston's journey from the desert of Arizona to the ice of Toronto proved that dreams could come true, regardless of where you come from. He taught us that age is just a number and that anyone can become a hero with hard work and dedication.

So, as you step onto the ice, remember Auston Matthews' story. Remember that every player starts as a rookie and has the potential to become a sensation with hard work and dedication.

This is just one of the many incredible stories of Rookie Sensations in the NHL. Our journey continues with more tales of young players who, like Auston Matthews, lit up the league with their talent and love for the game.

By Quintin Soloviev - Own work, CC BY-SA 4.0, https://commons.wikimedia.org/w/index.php?curid=124520861

YOUNG PLAYERS WHO CAPTURED HEARTS

Jonathan Toews was born on April 29, 1988, in Winnipeg, Manitoba, Canada. He had a hockey stick in his hand from the time he could walk, and his love for the game grew more and more each day. It quickly became apparent that he had a special connection with the ice.

Jonathan's father saw his son's passion and built a small rink in their backyard. It was a modest rink, but Jonathan would spend countless hours practicing his skills there. He would skate until his cheeks were rosy from the cold, honing his shots and perfecting his moves.

As Jonathan grew, so did his talent. His dedication and hard work paid off as he progressed through the youth hockey ranks. Known for his work ethic, it was clear that he was destined for greatness.

In 2006, the Chicago Blackhawks selected Jonathan in the NHL draft. At just 18 years old, he made his NHL debut, and his arrival was eagerly awaited.

As a rookie, Jonathan faced challenges in adjusting to the professional game. He was only 18 and had to adapt to the speed and physicality of the NHL. Additionally, he carried the weight of playing for a team with a long history of success and a dedicated fan base.

But Jonathan was not daunted by these challenges. He embraced them with a quiet determination that would become his trademark.

He was not the loudest voice in the locker room, but his actions spoke volumes. He worked tirelessly, both on and off the ice, earning the respect of his teammates and coaches.

In 2010, Jonathan was named the captain of the Chicago Blackhawks. He became one of the youngest captains in NHL history, but he proved he was more than ready for the challenge.

Under his leadership, the Blackhawks won the Stanley Cup in 2010, marking the beginning of a new era of success for the team. They would win two more Stanley Cups with Jonathan as their captain in 2013 and 2015.

Jonathan Toews is more than just a star on the ice; he is a true hero in Canadian hockey. He is a role model for aspiring players and young people nationwide. He is known for his sportsmanship, dedication to the game, and commitment to giving back to the community.

Jonathan Toews' journey is a testament to the power of dreams and the importance of hard work. He showed that you can make a significant impact in a small city. All you need is a love for the game and the determination to pursue your dreams.

Remember Jonathan Toews's story as you climb the ice and chase your dreams.

Remember that heroes can come from anywhere and inspire with their skill, character, and dedication to the game.

This is just one of the many incredible stories of young players who captured hearts in the NHL. Our journey continues with more tales of players who, like Jonathan Toews, became heroes through their passion for hockey and commitment to making a positive impact.

By Resolute - Own work, CC BY-SA 3.0, https://commons.wikimedia.org/w/index.php?curid=6598409

Trivia Fact	Player Name	Remarkable Achievement
Youngest Captain	Jonathan Toews	Became Chicago Blackhawks' captain at age 20.
Most Points by a Rookie	Wayne Gretzky	Scored 137 points in his rookie season (1979-1980).
The Rocket's Legacy	Maurice "Rocket" Richard	First player to score 50 goals in a single NHL season.
Gretzky's Assist Record	Wayne Gretzky	Recorded 163 assists in one NHL season (1985-1986).
The Great One's Scoring Titles	Wayne Gretzky	Won the Art Ross Trophy 10 times as the top scorer.
Maurice Richard's 8 Stanley Cups	Maurice "Rocket" Richard	Achieved 8 Stanley Cup wins, all with the Canadiens.
Sidney Crosby's Golden Goal	Sidney Crosby	Scored the game-winning goal in the 2010 Winter Olympics.
Youngest NHL Goalie	Patrick Roy	Became the youngest NHL goalie at age 20.
Original Six	Featuring Original Six players	Players from the era of the six original NHL teams.
Three Stanley Cups	Jonathan Toews	Led the Chi

4. PUCK DREAMS ON CANADIAN SOIL

- **Backyard Rinks and Frozen Ponds**
- **Learning to Skate and Shoot**
- **From Pick-Up Games to Organized Hockey**

BACKYARD RINKS AND FROZEN PONDS

In the charming town of Parry Sound, situated on the beautiful Georgian Bay in Ontario, a young boy named Bobby Orr was born and raised. Surrounded by breathtaking natural surroundings, the town was a perfect place for a future hockey legend to grow up.

Bobby's journey into the world of hockey began in his backyard. As the town was covered in snow every winter, Bobby's father, an ardent hockey enthusiast, would clear a section of their backyard and carefully flood it to make a makeshift rink. Although modest in size, the rink held endless possibilities. It was a place where Bobby's dreams began to take shape.Bobby would skate on the ice with skates that had seen generations of play. His father would guide him and impart the wisdom of the game. They would meticulously prepare the rink, ensuring the smooth ice and secure boards. The backyard rink became Bobby's canvas, where he would paint his dreams with every stride, shot, and save.

Weekends were a particular time for Bobby and his friends. They would go to the nearby frozen ponds, and Seguin River Pond was one of their favorite spots. The pond was a community gathering place where the ice stretched far and wide. Young players from Parry Sound and the surrounding areas would come together to play the game in its purest form.

The frozen pond was where the magic truly happened. Under the winter sun, they played from sunrise to sunset, their breath visible in the cold air. This was where friendships deepened, rivalries ignited, and the love for the game was cultivated. It was on that frozen canvas that Bobby and his friends began to understand the game's magic.

Bobby Orr was not only a talented skater and hockey player from a young age but a prodigy. He displayed a remarkable work ethic and an unwavering dedication to the game, values that would stay with him throughout his career.

As the years passed, Bobby's talent and dedication would elevate him from the backyard rink and frozen ponds of Parry Sound to the professional ice of the NHL. He became one of the greatest defensemen in the sport's history, a hero to young players across Canada.

Bobby Orr's achievements were nothing short of legendary. He won an astounding eight Stanley Cups, a feat that still stands as a record for defensemen. He was awarded three Norris Trophies as the NHL's best defenseman and two Hart Trophies as the league's most valuable player. Bobby Orr's name is etched in the annals of hockey history as one of the most influential and revered players the game has ever seen.

Bobby Orr's story is a testament to the power of backyard rinks and frozen ponds in shaping the dreams of Canadian hockey players. It's a story of hard work, dedication, and perseverance that continues to inspire young players on Canadian soil.

So, my young friend, as you lace up your skates and step onto the ice, remember the story of Bobby Orr and the countless others who, like him, began their journey on Canada's backyard rinks and frozen ponds. And this is just one of the many incredible stories from "Puck Dreams on Canadian Soil." Our journey continues with more tales of learning to skate, playing pick-up games, and transitioning to organized hockey.

Bobby Orr

LEARNING TO SKATE AND SHOOT

Born on October 5, 1965, in Quebec, Mario Lemieux's journey began in the heart of a province that has a deep-rooted passion for hockey. He would become one of Canada's most iconic players, and his path from learning to skate and shoot to becoming a hockey legend is a testament to his incredible talent and determination.

Mario's father, Jean-Guy Lemieux, a skilled hockey player, played a significant role in shaping his early years. Recognizing Mario's budding talent, he supported his love for the game. At the age of three, Mario took his first strides on the frozen ponds near his home in Ville-Émard, a suburb of Montreal.

Mario Lemieux

Attribution: By Tony McCune - Flickr: Mario Lemieux, Hall of Famer, CC BY 2.0,
https://commons.wikimedia.org/w/index.php?curid=30300081

His father guided him through the process, and what made Mario's skating style unique was his long, graceful strides and his ability to skate backward with ease.

Mario's father also understood the importance of a powerful and accurate shot, so he built a small rink in their backyard where Mario could hone his skills. His ability to shoot from anywhere on the ice became a defining characteristic of his game.

His father guided him through the process, and what made Mario's skating style unique was his long, graceful strides and his ability to skate backward with ease. Mario's father also understood the importance of a powerful and accurate shot, so he built a small rink in their backyard where Mario could hone his skills. His ability to shoot from anywhere on the ice became a defining characteristic of his game.

Mario's passion and talent became evident to all who watched him play as he continued to grow. At age four, he was already playing organized hockey, dazzling teammates and opponents with his exceptional skills.

In 1984, the Pittsburgh Penguins drafted Mario with the first overall pick in the NHL Entry Draft, a testament to his extraordinary talent. He quickly became one of the league's top players, winning two Stanley Cups with the Penguins in 1991 and 1992. His career was marked by incredible achievements and records, showcasing his extraordinary shot power, accuracy, and skating prowess.

Even after retiring from the NHL in 1997, Mario couldn't resist the game's call. He returned to play for the Penguins from 2000 to 2006, further solidifying his status as a hockey legend. He finally retired for good in 2006, leaving behind a legacy that continues to inspire young Canadian hockey players.

As you embark on learning to skate and shoot, remember the story of Mario Lemieux. You, too, can take your love for the game from the backyard rinks and frozen ponds to the grand arenas of professional hockey. The key is dedication and a love for the game.

This is just one of the many incredible stories from "Puck Dreams on Canadian Soil." Our journey continues with more pick-up game tales and the transition to organized hockey.

FROM PICK-UP GAMES TO ORGANIZED HOCKEY

Joe Sakic, a boy born on July 7, 1969, in Burnaby, British Columbia, is the epitome of Canada's love for hockey. His journey from playing pick-up games on frozen ponds to becoming a hockey legend proves that passion and dedication can take you a long way.

Joe's story began like many young Canadian boys, playing pick-up games on impromptu rinks. His father, Marijan Sakic, was a Croatian immigrant who embraced Canada's national sport. Joe and his friends spent countless hours playing casual games in their backyard, complete with makeshift boards, and feeling the exhilaration of scoring goals.

Joe's natural talent was evident from a young age. His precision in shooting, exceptional skating skills, and ability to read the ice made him stand out. At age five, he joined a local team to play organized hockey, marking the transition from informal rinks to structured play.

This transition was a pivotal step in Joe's journey. He quickly made a name for himself as a promising young player, consistently delivering standout performances. His remarkable skating style, characterized by long strides and quick direction changes, caught the attention of scouts.

By age 16, Joe Sakic had already made a mark in the Western Hockey League (WHL), playing for the Swift Current Broncos.

In 1987, he was selected by the Quebec Nordiques in the NHL Entry Draft, where he made his professional debut in 1988. Joe quickly established himself as one of the league's top players.

Joe Sakic's father, Marijan, played a significant role in his development as a player. He emphasized the importance of efficient backward skating and the art of shooting with power and precision from any position on the ice. Joe developed a unique skating style marked by long, graceful strides and quick direction changes. His immediate release and scoring prowess became his trademarks.

Joe Sakic's journey is a reminder that even the most significant players started on humble pick-up rinks. With dedication and the right opportunities, dreams can indeed become a reality. His story continues to inspire young Canadian players, showing them that a love for the game and hard work can take them from the neighborhood rink to the grand stage of the NHL.

Joe Sakic

Trivia Fact	Description
Wayne Gretzky's Backyard Rink	Wayne Gretzky's father, Walter Gretzky, built a backyard rink in Brantford, Ontario, where Wayne practiced his skills, setting the stage for his legendary career.
Frozen Ponds of Quebec	Many future NHL stars from Quebec, like Mario Lemieux, spent their childhood on frozen ponds, developing their love for the game.
Joe Sakic's Croatian Heritage	Joe Sakic's father, Marijan Sakic, brought his love for hockey from Croatia and passed it on to Joe, emphasizing the importance of skating and shooting skills.
Sidney Crosby's Childhood Rink	Sidney Crosby, a native of Cole Harbour, Nova Scotia, practiced on a backyard rink, honing his skills from an early age.
The Backyard Rinks of Manitoba	Manitoba has produced numerous hockey greats, including Jonathan Toews, who, like many others, began playing on backyard rinks in the province.
The Role of Fathers	Many of these young Canadian players were introduced to the game by their fathers, who played a crucial role in their early development.
Joe Sakic's WHL Journey	Joe Sakic's time in the Western Hockey League (WHL) with the Swift Current Broncos was a significant stepping stone toward his NHL career.
Wayne Gretzky's Early Skating	Wayne Gretzky first learned to skate at the age of two under the guidance of his father, setting him on a path to become the "Great One."
Early NHL Draft Selections	Several of these players were drafted into the NHL at a young age, showcasing their immense talent and potential to excel at the professional level.
The Community Spirit of Hockey	Pick-up games on frozen ponds and backyard rinks fostered a sense of community and camaraderie that still resonates in the hearts of many Canadian hockey players.
Hockey's Indigenous Roots	The sport of ice hockey is believed to have originated in Canada, with Indigenous peoples playing a precursor of the game for centuries.
The Birth of the NHL	The National Hockey League (NHL), one of the world's premier hockey leagues, was founded in Montreal, Quebec, in 1917.
Original Six Teams	The NHL's "Original Six" consisted of the Boston Bruins, Chicago Blackhawks, Detroit Red Wings, Montreal Canadiens, New York Rangers, and Toronto Maple Leafs.
Wayne Gretzky's Records	Wayne Gretzky holds numerous NHL records, including most career goals, assists, and points. His nickname, "The Great One," reflects his incredible career.

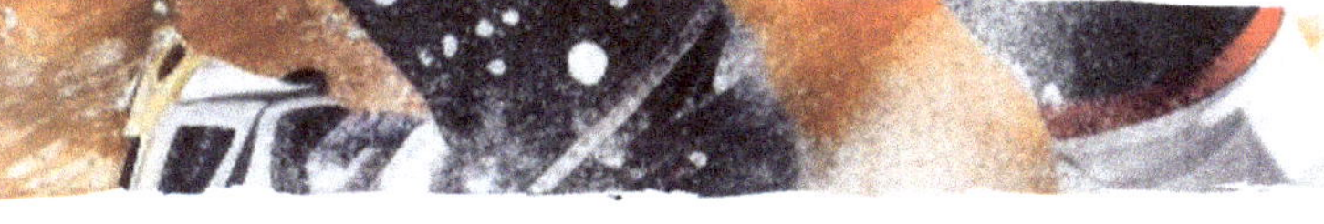

5. THE SPIRIT OF CANADIAN HOCKEY

- Values and Traditions of the Game
- Sportsmanship and Teamwork
- The Role of Coaches and Mentors

VALUES AND TRADITIONS OF THE GAME

A young boy named Gordie Howe lived in the heart of small-town Saskatchewan. It was a community where hockey was not just a sport but a way of life. Kids like Gordie were introduced to the game at an early age, and the rink was where they learned valuable life lessons that would stay with them forever.

Gordie's story is a testament to Canadian hockey's core values and traditions. His passion for the game ignited when he began skating with the neighborhood kids on the frozen fields and ponds. But it wasn't just about scoring goals but respect, sportsmanship, and camaraderie.

In those days, young players were taught to play hard but fair. They learned the importance of shaking hands with their opponents, win or lose. They knew that the game was more significant than any player and that teamwork was the foundation of success. Gordie's parents, Ab and Katie Howe instilled in him a strong work ethic and humility. They emphasized giving back to the community and being a positive role model. These were values that Gordie carried with him throughout his legendary career.

Gordie faced challenges and obstacles as he progressed in the sport but remained persistent in his commitment to the game's traditions. He treated teammates, opponents, and fans with respect and kindness. He played the game with passion and a sense of responsibility, understanding that he was a steward of the sport.

Gordie Howe became one of the greatest players in hockey history, earning the nickname "Mr. Hockey."He embodied the values and traditions of the game, and his legacy continues to inspire young players across Canada.

Gordie Howe's legacy is about more than just his on-ice accomplishments. He was also a role model off the ice, known for his sportsmanship, commitment to community service, and dedication to his family.The Gordie Howe Foundation, which he established with his wife Colleen in 2002, provides financial assistance to underprivileged youth so that they can participate in hockey. The foundation also supports programs that promote sportsmanship, teamwork, and leadership.

Gordie Howe's impact on Canadian hockey is immeasurable. He was a true champion of the game, and his legacy continues to shape the future of Canadian hockey. Gordie Howe exemplified Canadian hockey's values and traditions, leaving a remarkable legacy of sportsmanship, respect, and giving back to the community.

His story serves as a shining example of the spirit of Canadian hockey, reminding young players that the true essence of the game is not just in the goals scored but in the lessons learned along the way. Gordie Howe's legacy is an enduring symbol of what it means to be a Canadian hockey hero.

Gordie Howe

SPORTSMANSHIP AND TEAMWORK

Once upon a time, in the bustling city of Montreal, a young boy named Jean Béliveau loved hockey and had remarkable skills on the ice. Jean was known for his sportsmanship, excellent teamwork, and respect for his opponents.

Jean's parents taught him the importance of essential values such as respect, kindness, and working together. They believed hockey was about scoring goals and playing with heart and soul for both the team and opponents.

Jean grew up playing for teams like the Quebec Citadelles and the Quebec Aces, where he honed his skills and sportsmanship. In 1953, Jean joined the Montreal Canadiens, where he became known for his outstanding play and leadership skills. He helped his team win several Stanley Cups and earned the title of Captain Jean Béliveau.

In 1971, the Canadiens won the Stanley Cup, and Jean did something remarkable. Instead of being the first to lift the trophy, he gave it to his teammate and friend, Henri Richard. This act of selflessness demonstrates the importance of teamwork and sportsmanship.

Even after retiring from playing, Jean continued to serve hockey as an ambassador, traveling around and reminding young players about the significance of playing fair, being a good sport, and sticking together.

Jean Béliveau's story is an inspiring journey through the heart of Canadian hockey.

It teaches us that winning is not everything, but how we play the game with fairness, kindness, and the best team spirit ever. Remember Jean Béliveau when you play your games and strive to be a great teammate, show sportsmanship, and who knows, maybe one day, you'll be a legend too!

Jean Béliveau

THE ROLE OF COACHES AND MENTORS

Clare Drake was a legendary coach and mentor in Canadian hockey history, hailing from Yorkton, Saskatchewan. Growing up in the prairies, he understood that hockey wasn't just a sport but a way of life. His early experiences on the ice shaped his deep understanding of the values and traditions of Canadian hockey.

Clare's journey as a coach and mentor began at a young age when he discovered his passion for the game. He played for the Golden Bears at the University of Alberta and transitioned into coaching after playing. As a coach, he emphasized respect, teamwork, and sportsmanship, teaching his players that hockey was a team sport and success came from working together as a cohesive unit.

Under his guidance, the University of Alberta's Golden Bears became a powerhouse, winning numerous national championships. But Clare's influence extended beyond the rink; he emphasized the importance of education, character development, and community involvement.

Clare Drake's legacy as a coach and mentor extended to the national stage. He coached the Canadian national team at the World Championships and the Olympics, where he continued to instill the values of Canadian hockey in a new generation of players.

In 2018, Clare Drake was inducted into the Hockey Hall of Fame, not as a player, but as a builder of the sport. It was a testament to his impact on the sport's values and traditions. Clare Drake's story is a reminder that coaches and mentors play a pivotal role in shaping the spirit of Canadian hockey.

Their influence extends far beyond the wins and losses; it's about molding young players into skilled athletes and respectful, responsible, and sportsmanlike individuals.

Clare Drake was also a strong advocate for women's hockey, having coached the Canadian women's national team in the early 1980s when the sport was less prevalent than it is today.

Today, young Canadian players follow in the footsteps of Clare Drake, who carried the torch of Canadian hockey's values and traditions. Coaches and mentors like him are the unsung heroes behind every great player, quietly shaping the future of the sport one lesson at a time. Clare Drake was a true pioneer of Canadian hockey, a coach and mentor who made a lasting impact on the sport and its players. His legacy continues to inspire coaches and young athletes alike.

Clare Drake

#	Trivia Fact
1	The Stanley Cup, awarded to the NHL champions, was first presented in 1893.
2	The first organized indoor hockey game was played in Montreal in 1875.
3	The oldest amateur hockey organization in North America, the Montreal Amateur Athletic Association (MAAA), was founded in 1887.
4	Wayne Gretzky, often considered one of the greatest hockey players of all time, holds numerous NHL records, including most career points and assists.
5	The Hockey Hall of Fame, located in Toronto, Canada, was established in 1943 to honor the history of hockey.
6	Canada has won more Olympic gold medals in ice hockey than any other country.
7	The "Original Six" refers to the six original NHL teams before expansion: the Montreal Canadiens, Toronto Maple Leafs, Boston Bruins, Detroit Red Wings, Chicago Black Hawks (now Blackhawks), and New York Rangers.
8	The first recorded women's hockey game took place in 1892 in Ottawa, Canada.
9	Bobby Orr, a legendary defenseman, won the Norris Trophy (awarded to the NHL's best defenseman) a record eight times.
10	Canada's iconic "Hockey Night in Canada" broadcast began in 1952 and remains a beloved tradition for fans across the country.

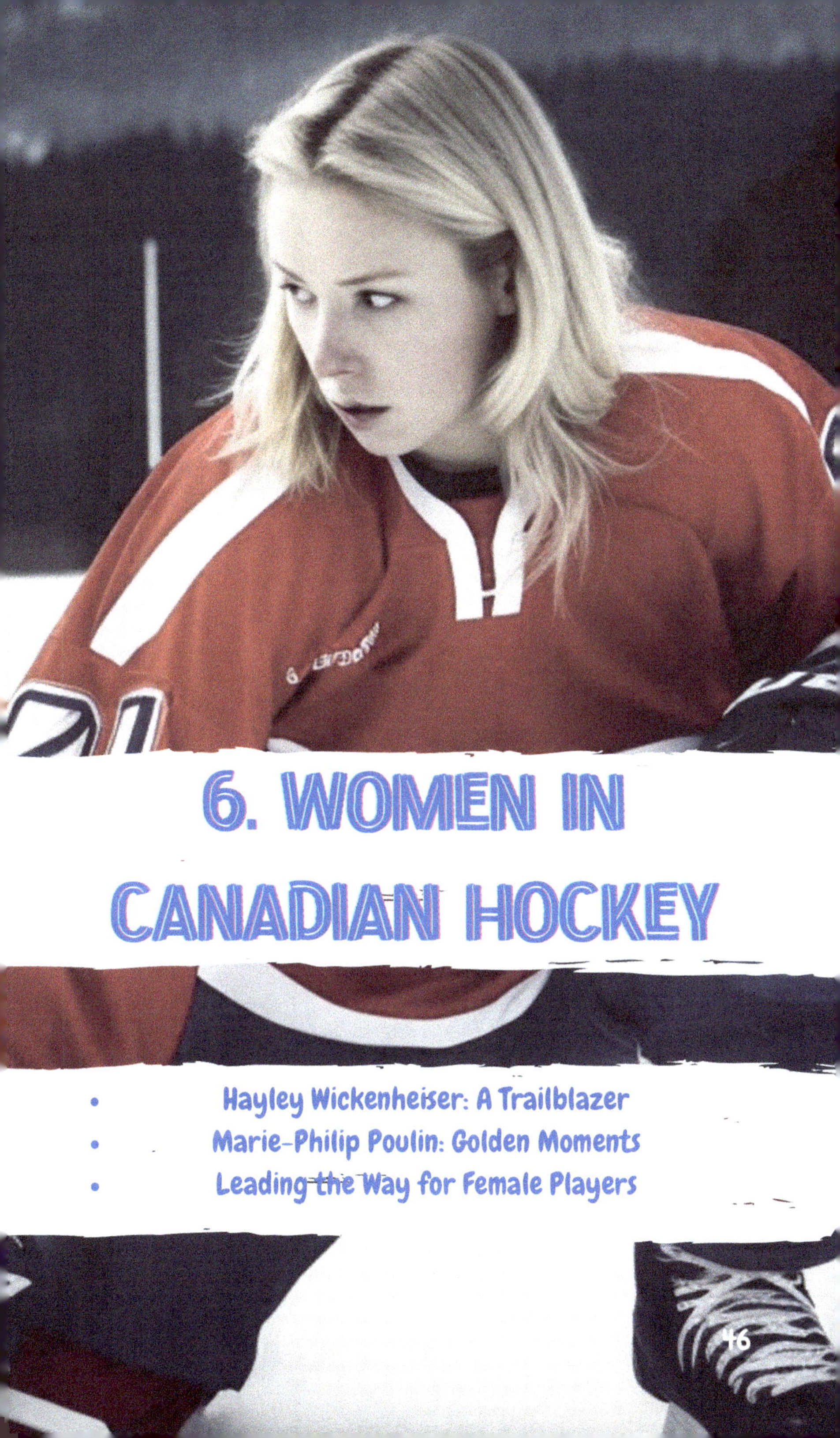

6. WOMEN IN CANADIAN HOCKEY

- Hayley Wickenheiser: A Trailblazer
- Marie-Philip Poulin: Golden Moments
- Leading the Way for Female Players

HAYLEY WICKENHEISER: A TRAILBLAZER

Hayley Wickenheiser grew up in Shaunavon, Saskatchewan, where she developed a passion for hockey at a young age. Despite facing the challenge of playing in a predominantly male sport, she remained dedicated and resilient. She played in boys' leagues and became a skilled and fearless player. Her talent and determination caught the attention of scouts, and at the age of 15, she joined the Women's Western Hockey League's Swift Current Wildcats.

Hayley quickly gained recognition for her incredible skills, speed on the ice, and unwavering commitment to the game. She debuted for the national team at age 15 and became a key player in pioneering the Canadian women's national team. She helped secure numerous gold medals for Canada at the IIHF Women's World Championships and the Winter Olympics. Her remarkable career spanned over two decades, and she earned her place among the most outstanding female hockey players ever.

Hayley's story goes beyond her success. She became a trailblazer for female players in Canada, inspiring generations to follow their dreams in the sport they love. She consistently emphasized the importance of equality in sports and the need for more opportunities for female athletes. She advocated for change, pushing for better facilities, resources, and support for women's hockey.

Off the ice, Hayley's legacy as a trailblazer continues. She has transitioned into a medical career while remaining connected to the sport. She was inducted into the Hockey Hall of Fame for her remarkable achievements on the ice and her unwavering dedication to improving the landscape of women's hockey.

Hayley Wickenheiser's journey is a shining example of what can be achieved through passion, hard work, and a commitment to breaking barriers. Her legacy is felt on the ice and in the hearts of countless young Canadian girls who now dare to dream of playing hockey at the highest level.

Hayley's story is a testament to the changing face of Canadian hockey. She showed that with determination and perseverance, young Canadian girls can follow their hearts and carve out their path, making their mark in a sport once dominated by men. She's not just a trailblazer; she's an inspiration for future generations.

Hayley Wickenheiser

MARIE-PHILIP POULIN: GOLDEN MOMENTS

Marie-Philip Poulin, a young girl from the charming town of Beauceville, Quebec, discovered her love for hockey early on. She became one of the most celebrated and accomplished Canadian women's hockey players, leaving behind a legacy of golden moments that have inspired countless young players.

Born on March 28, 1991, Marie-Philip's destiny as a hockey star began to take shape when she stepped onto the ice. Her passion for the game was evident, and she quickly became an elite player.

Marie-Philip's list of accomplishments in hockey is nothing short of astounding. She is undoubtedly one of Canadian history's most successful and celebrated female hockey players with four Olympic gold medals and seven world championship gold medals. Her induction into the Hockey Hall of Fame is a testament to her incredible career and impact on the sport.

One of Marie-Philip's first notable achievements came when she was just 18 years old. In the 2009 IIHF Women's World Championship, she played a pivotal role in helping Team Canada secure a gold medal. Her standout performance in the tournament earned her the title of Top Forward, and her game-winning goal in the final against the United States demonstrated her ability to shine on the world stage.

However, in the 2010 Winter Olympics, Marie-Philip Poulin etched her name in the annals of hockey history. Facing off against their arch-rivals, the United States in the gold medal game, Canada was trailing 2-0 late in the third period.

But in a dramatic turn of events, Marie-Philip scored not one but two goals, including the game-tying goal with just 55 seconds remaining. She then added the game-winner in overtime, securing Canada's gold medal and cementing her status as a national hero.

The "Golden Goal," as it came to be known, was a defining moment in Canadian hockey history. Marie-Philip's poise, skill, and determination under pressure captured the hearts of a nation. Her heroics in the 2010 Olympics were especially significant as they took place on Canadian soil in Vancouver.

Marie-Philip Poulin's brilliance on the ice continued to shine in subsequent years. She won more gold medals with Team Canada in the Olympics and the Women's World Championships, further solidifying her place as one of the greatest female hockey players ever.Off the ice, Marie-Philip became a role model for young Canadian players, especially girls aspiring to make their mark in a sport traditionally dominated by men. She is a spokesperson for several youth hockey programs and regularly visits schools and community events to inspire young people.

Marie-Philip Poulin

Marie-Philip Poulin's golden moments have brought glory to Canadian women's hockey and inspired generations of young athletes.

Her extraordinary talent and her ability to perform under pressure are qualities that all aspiring players can look up to and strive to emulate. She is a true Canadian hockey icon, and her legacy continues to inspire young players, demonstrating that they, too, can create golden moments of their own in the great game of hockey.

LEADING THE WAY FOR FEMALE PLAYERS

In 1998, a group of determined young girls from Mississauga, Ontario, laced up their skates to showcase their skills on the ice. They were the Mississauga Chiefs and would become trailblazers for female players in Canadian hockey.

Coach Dan Cassidy was a visionary who recognized the potential of female players and believed in their right to compete at the highest level. He was instrumental in establishing the Ontario Women's Hockey Association, which aimed to provide a structured league for young female players. This was a monumental step towards creating opportunities for girls to play organized hockey.

Despite the limited opportunities and resources available to female players in the late 1990s, the Mississauga Chiefs became a dominant force in the league, winning numerous provincial championships and inspiring a generation of young female players.

One of the key figures in this remarkable journey was Jayna Hefford, a gifted player with a passion for the game that was second to none. She was a leading scorer for the Chiefs.

The legacy of the Mississauga Chiefs extended beyond their on-ice achievements. They inspired a generation of young female players who aspired to follow in their footsteps. Their success helped to change the landscape of female hockey in Canada. It showed that with dedication, talent, and a robust support system, there are no limits to what young female players can achieve in Canadian hockey.

Today, Canadian female hockey players from the grassroots to the professional level owe a debt of gratitude to the Mississauga Chiefs and their visionary coach, Dan Cassidy. Their journey serves as a reminder of the incredible progress made in the world of women's hockey. It continues to inspire and motivate girls across the nation to lace up their skates, chase their dreams, and push the boundaries of the sport they love.

Cherie Piper

Title	Trivia Fact
Hayley Wickenheiser: A Trailblazer	Hayley Wickenheiser was the first female hockey player to receive a full scholarship to a Canadian university.
Hayley Wickenheiser: A Trailblazer	Hayley Wickenheiser is the all-time leading scorer in women's international hockey history.
Marie-Philip Poulin: Golden Moments	Marie-Philip Poulin scored the game-winning goal in overtime to lead Canada to a gold medal at the 2010 Winter Olympics.
Marie-Philip Poulin: Golden Moments	Marie-Philip Poulin is the only player in Olympic history to score two game-winning goals in overtime in the gold medal game.
Leading the Way for Female Players	The Mississauga Chiefs were one of the first female hockey teams in Canada to play in an organized league.
Leading the Way for Female Players	The Mississauga Chiefs inspired a generation of young female hockey players, including Jayna Hefford, who would go on to become one of Canada's most celebrated female hockey players.
Women in Canadian Hockey	Canada has won more gold medals at the IIHF Women's World Championship than any other country.
Women in Canadian Hockey	Canada has won four consecutive Olympic gold medals in women's hockey.
Women in Canadian Hockey	Canadian women's hockey players have won over 200 Olympic and world championship medals.
Women in Canadian Hockey	The first women's hockey game was played in Canada in 1892.
Women in Canadian Hockey	The first women's hockey league in Canada was founded in 1923.

7. OVERCOMING CHALLENGES

- Triumph in the Face of Adversity
- Stories of Resilience and Determination
- When the Going Gets Tough

TRIUMPH IN THE FACE OF ADVERSITY

Bryan Berard, a name that holds a special place in the history of Canadian hockey, was born in Woonsocket, Rhode Island. However, his passion for the sport began in Plattsville, Ontario - a small town. His journey in hockey was remarkable, and he achieved a lot of accomplishments that most young players only dream of.

Berard was a gifted defenseman, and his success came quickly. The Ottawa Senators selected him first overall in the 1995 NHL Entry Draft, and he immediately showcased his skills on the ice. Berard earned two All-Star selections and won a gold medal with Team Canada at the 1997 World Junior Championships. His future in hockey seemed destined for greatness.

But, during his time with the Toronto Maple Leafs, Berard's story took an unexpected and challenging turn. In the 2000-2001 season, he suffered a severe injury when his teammate Marian Hossa's high stick struck his right eye. The injury was so powerful that Berard had to undergo seven surgeries, leaving him with permanently impaired vision in his right eye. Many thought that his hockey career was over, and his journey to recovery was marked with uncertainty and doubt.

However, Bryan Berard's unyielding determination sets him apart from others. He refused to let adversity define his story. With sheer willpower and unwavering support from his family and teammates, he made an astonishing comeback to the NHL, signing with the New York Rangers.In 2002, Berard's return to professional hockey was nothing short of a miracle. He wore a specially designed contact lens to correct his vision, defying the odds and proving that determination can overcome even the most challenging circumstances.

His comeback inspired hockey fans across the globe.In 2004, Bryan Berard's resilience and incredible journey were recognized when he was awarded the Bill Masterton Trophy. This prestigious honor is presented annually to the NHL player who best exemplifies perseverance, sportsmanship, and dedication to hockey.

Berard's triumph in the face of adversity remains an inspiring chapter in the history of Canadian hockey. His story is a testament to the power of the human spirit and the unwavering love for hockey. His legacy motivates young Canadians to overcome life's challenges and pursue their dreams with courage and resilience. Bryan Berard's journey is a vivid reminder that even in the darkest times, there is always a glimmer of hope - a lesson he shares with every aspiring young player who faces adversity.

Bryan Berard

STORIES OF RESILIENCE AND DETERMINATION

A young boy named Mario Lemieux was born on October 5, 1965, in Montreal, Quebec. His outstanding skills in hockey were evident from a very young age. Lemieux played junior hockey for the Laval Voisins in his hometown, where his electrifying play and effortless skating made him a fan favorite. 1984, the Pittsburgh Penguins selected him first in the NHL Entry Draft.

As a Penguin, Lemieux quickly became one of the league's most dominant players. Standing tall at 6'4", his size, speed, skill, and hockey IQ made him virtually unstoppable. He earned six Art Ross Trophies as the NHL's leading scorer and two Hart Trophies as the NHL's most valuable player.

However, adversity struck just as his career was reaching its pinnacle. In 1993, Lemieux was diagnosed with Hodgkin's lymphoma, a form of cancer. It was a devastating blow to both Lemieux and the hockey community. Nevertheless, Lemieux faced this challenge with the same determination and courage that defined his play on the ice.

While battling cancer, Lemieux underwent grueling treatment and recovery, which forced him to miss most of the 1993-94 NHL season. It was a dark period, but he never lost sight of his dream to return to the game he loved.

In 1994-95, Lemieux made a triumphant comeback to the NHL. His return was nothing short of remarkable. He scored 69 goals and registered 161 points in just 70 games, leading the Pittsburgh Penguins to the Stanley Cup championship. He was awarded the Conn Smythe Trophy as the playoff MVP.

Lemieux's story teaches us that anything is possible without giving up on our dreams. It also shows us the power of the human spirit and the importance of resilience in the face of challenges. His triumph over adversity is an inspiration to us all.

Lemieux's legacy extends far beyond his accomplishments on the ice. He is a role model for all who face adversity. His story reminds us that we can overcome obstacles and achieve our goals with courage, determination, and a never-give-up attitude.

In 1993, Lemieux founded the Mario Lemieux Foundation, which supports cancer research and patient care. His commitment to giving back to the community is admirable.

Mario Lemieux

WHEN THE GOING GETS TOUGH

Paul Kariya, a young boy from Vancouver, British Columbia, had a passion for hockey from an early age and was a talented player on the ice. He played junior hockey for the University of Maine, winning the Hobey Baker Award twice and leading the team to a national championship in 1993.

Paul's professional career began when he was selected fourth overall by the Anaheim Ducks in the 1993 NHL Entry Draft. He quickly became one of the league's brightest stars, known for his speed, playmaking abilities, and fearlessness. He won the Lady Byng Trophy twice in his first two NHL seasons for sportsmanship and skill.

In 1997, during a game against the Chicago Blackhawks, Paul suffered a brutal open-ice hit from Gary Suter, resulting in a concussion that could have ended his career. However, he persevered through months of recovery and rehabilitation and made a remarkable comeback in 1998, continuing to dominate on the ice.

Throughout his illustrious career, Paul was a seven-time NHL All-Star, scored over 100 points in a season twice, and represented Canada at the World Junior Championships and the Winter Olympics, winning a gold medal and a silver medal, respectively.

Paul's contributions extended beyond his playing career. He made a generous donation to the University of Maine, which resulted in naming their ice arena after him. He is now a Hockey Hall of Fame member and a true Canadian hockey hero.

Paul Kariya's inspiring story teaches us that we can overcome adversity and achieve our dreams with unwavering determination and a love for the game.

Paul Kariya

Topic	Fact/Trivia
1972 Summit Series	The Canadian team trailed 3-1 but won the last three games to win the series overall.
1980 Miracle on Ice	The US hockey team defeated the heavily favored Soviet Union team.
1996 World Cup of Hockey	The Canadian team lost their first two games but won the next five to win the championship.
2002 Winter Olympics	The Canadian women's hockey team defeated the US team to win the gold medal.
2010 Winter Olympics	The Canadian men's hockey team defeated the US team to win the gold medal.
Mario Lemieux	Returned to the NHL less than a year after being diagnosed with Hodgkin's lymphoma and led the Pittsburgh Penguins to the Stanley Cup championship in 1993.
Paul Kariya	Made a remarkable comeback in 1998 after suffering a severe concussion.
Steve Yzerman	Played through a variety of injuries throughout his career, including a broken nose, a concussion, and a torn ACL. He also suffered the loss of his father to cancer during his rookie season.
2010 Canadian Olympic women's hockey team	Made up of players from all over Canada, from different backgrounds and walks of life. They came together as a team and won the gold medal, inspiring Canadians everywhere.
Every young hockey player	Dreams of one day playing in the NHL. For many, that dream is shattered by injuries or other challenges. But for a few lucky ones, the dream comes true.

8. THE FUTURE STARS

- Rising Young Talent in Canadian Hockey
- Dreams of Playing in the NHL
- Aspiring to Follow in Legends' Footsteps

RISING YOUNG TALENT IN CANADIAN HOCKEY

In the heart of Richmond Hill, Ontario, a young boy named Connor McDavid lifted his skates and took to the ice. It was evident from a very early age that he was no ordinary hockey player. By the time he was a teenager, Connor was already being compared to some of the greatest names in the sport. He possessed an uncanny ability to read the game, showcasing unparalleled speed and extraordinary puck-handling skills. The future of Canadian hockey was taking its first strides on those rinks.

Connor's incredible journey continued as he rose through the Ontario Hockey League (OHL) ranks. He joined the Erie Otters, and his impact was immediate. He set numerous records and led the league in scoring, showing the world that a new superstar was in the making.

In 2015, the hockey world watched with bated breath as Connor McDavid's name was called as the first overall pick in the NHL Entry Draft. The Edmonton Oilers had secured a generational talent with sky-high expectations.

His rookie season was nothing short of remarkable. Although he wasn't named captain immediately, he quickly proved himself as a leader on and off the ice.

Connor's incredible speed, scoring ability, and playmaking skills wowed fans and experts.

 He won the Art Ross Trophy multiple times as the NHL's leading scorer, earning a spot on the NHL First All-Star Team. His impact on the Oilers and the entire league was undeniable.

But what sets Connor McDavid apart is his talent and character. He leads by example, displaying sportsmanship, humility, and a tireless work ethic. He has become a role model for young players across Canada, inspiring them to chase their dreams with unwavering dedication.

As the years have passed, Connor McDavid's legacy has continued to grow. He is more than just a hockey player; he symbolizes what is possible with talent, hard work, and the support of a loving family and community. He represents the future of Canadian hockey, and his story reminds us all that dreams can be achieved with dedication and determination. Connor McDavid's meteoric rise from a young boy in Richmond Hill to a hockey superstar inspires us all, and his journey is far from over.

Connor McDavid

DREAMS OF PLAYING IN THE NHL

Pernell-Karl Subban, or P.K., grew up in Toronto, Ontario, with a love for hockey and a dream of becoming a great player. He quickly showed his skills as a defenseman with an impressive offensive game and rose through the youth hockey ranks.

P.K. was dedicated to the sport and worked tirelessly to improve his skills. His hard work paid off in 2007 when the Montreal Canadiens selected him in the second round of the NHL Entry Draft. He debuted his NHL in the 2009-2010 season and quickly became a fan favorite due to his exciting and dynamic playing style.

P.K.'s dedication to the sport paid off, as he was named to the NHL All-Rookie Team in his first season. He continued to succeed throughout his career, winning the Calder Trophy as the league's top rookie in the 2010-2011 season and being named an NHL All-Star three times. In 2013, he won the Norris Trophy as the league's best defenseman.

In addition to his success on the ice, P.K. has significantly impacted the ice through his philanthropic work. In 2015, he generously donated to the Montreal Children's Hospital, resulting in the hospital's atrium being named after him in honor of his commitment to the community. He also founded the P.K. Subban Foundation, which provides educational and athletic opportunities for underserved youth, making a lasting difference in the lives of young Canadians.

P.K.'s journey from a young hockey enthusiast to an NHL superstar is a testament to the power of hard work, dedication, and belief in one's dreams.

His story inspires young Canadians everywhere, reminding them they can make their dreams come true with relentless effort and determination. Furthermore, P.K. is a role model for his commitment to giving back to the community and positively impacting the world.

Pernell-Karl Subban

ASPIRING TO FOLLOW IN LEGENDS' FOOTSTEPS

In the picturesque town of Cole Harbour, Nova Scotia, a young boy named Nathan MacKinnon had a dream. He was inspired by Canadian hockey legends and determined to make his mark in the sport. From an early age, it was clear that Nathan had a remarkable talent for hockey that would take him far.

Like many young Canadians, Nathan began his hockey journey by skating on frozen ponds and practicing in frigid temperatures. His skills quickly emerged, and he became well-known in his local community. By age 8, he was already impressing spectators with his speed, agility, and intuitive understanding of the game.

His exceptional skills became increasingly evident as Nathan progressed through the youth hockey ranks. He led his teams to numerous victories, earning widespread recognition and praise. His reputation as a young prodigy began to spread far beyond the confines of Cole Harbour.

In 2011, Nathan was selected as the first overall pick in the QMJHL Entry Draft by the Halifax Mooseheads of the Quebec Major Junior Hockey League (QMJHL). He continued to dazzle hockey fans with his impressive performances and captured the hearts of many.

Nathan's next major milestone was being selected as the first overall pick in the 2013 NHL Entry Draft by the Colorado Avalanche. The Avalanche saw in him the potential to carry on the legacy of Canadian hockey greatness, and Nathan was determined to prove himself on the NHL stage. Throughout his career, Nathan MacKinnon has achieved numerous milestones.

He's been named an NHL All-Star, won the Calder Trophy as the league's top rookie, and led the Avalanche to the Stanley Cup Final twice. His incredible speed, relentless determination, and unwavering sportsmanship have made him one of the NHL's most beloved and respected players.

Off the ice, Nathan is more than just a hockey star. He's known for his charitable work and commitment to community service. He actively participates in various philanthropic initiatives, including the Nathan MacKinnon Foundation, which supports children's healthcare and education. Nathan is also a role model for young hockey players and often participates in events and clinics to help them develop their skills and understand the importance of hard work and dedication.

Nathan MacKinnon's story is an inspiration to young Canadians everywhere. He is a shining example of what can be achieved through hard work, dedication, and a belief in one's dreams. Nathan's journey is a reminder that anything is possible if you set your mind to it and never give up.

Nathan MacKinnon

Topic	Fact/Trivia
Rising Young Talent in Canadian Hockey	Connor McDavid is the youngest captain in NHL history.
	Shane Wright is the first overall pick in the 2022 NHL Entry Draft.
	Mason McTavish is the third overall pick in the 2021 NHL Entry Draft.
	Owen Power is the first overall pick in the 2021 NHL Entry Draft.
	Juraj Slafkovsky is the first overall pick in the 2022 NHL Entry Draft.
Dreams of Playing in the NHL	97% of NHL players played in minor hockey.
	The average age of an NHL player is 27 years old.
	There are 32 teams in the NHL.
	The NHL is the most popular professional hockey league in the world.
	The Stanley Cup is the oldest and most prestigious trophy in North American professional sports.
Aspiring to Follow in Legends' Footsteps	Sidney Crosby is the youngest player to win the Stanley Cup as captain.
	Wayne Gretzky is the NHL's all-time leading scorer.
	Mario Lemieux is the NHL's all-time leading scorer in goals per game.
	Bobby Orr is the NHL's all-time leading scorer in assists per game.
	Gordie Howe is the NHL's all-time leading scorer in games played.

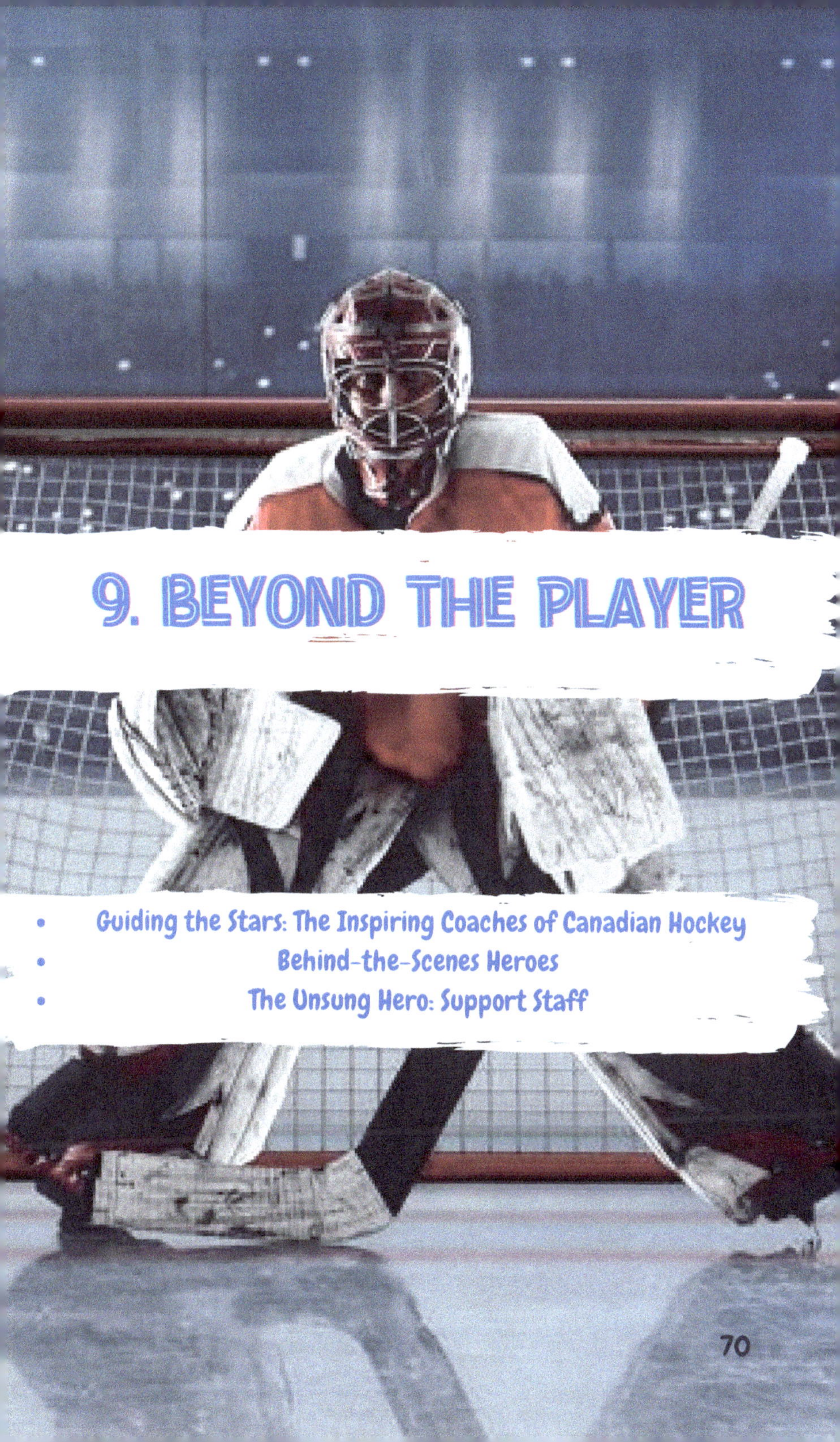

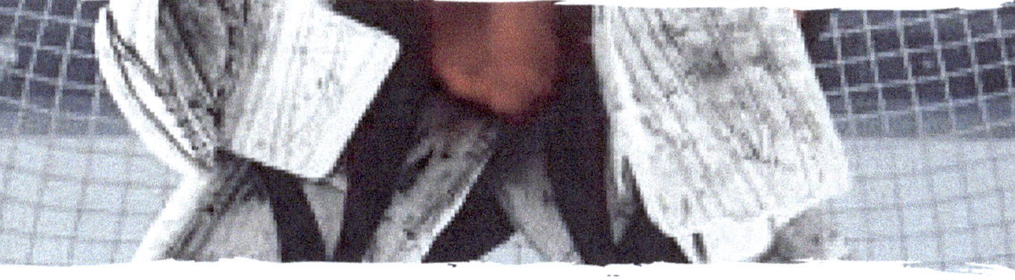

9. BEYOND THE PLAYER

- Guiding the Stars: The Inspiring Coaches of Canadian Hockey
- Behind-the-Scenes Heroes
- The Unsung Hero: Support Staff

THE INSPIRING COACHES OF CANADIAN HOCKEY

In Canada's hockey world, coaches are often the unsung heroes who work behind the scenes and shape the future of the sport by mentoring players. These coaches, who are dedicated and passionate about the game, leave a lasting impression on the players they guide. This is the inspiring story of a coach who made an indelible mark on Canadian hockey, Pat Quinn.

Pat Quinn, a towering figure both in physical stature and in the hockey world, was born on January 29, 1943, in Hamilton, Ontario. Although his playing career as a defenseman in the NHL was remarkable, his journey as a coach truly made him an icon. Quinn's career started with the Edmonton Oil Kings in junior hockey, where he won the Memorial Cup in 1963, which foreshadowed his future coaching success.

Quinn made his NHL coaching debut with the Philadelphia Flyers in 1979. His leadership behind the bench was evident as he guided the Flyers to an incredible 35-game unbeaten streak. This record still stands unmatched in any significant professional sport in North America. This exceptional achievement demonstrated his coaching prowess and ability to inspire and lead a team to greatness. However, Quinn's work as an international coach cemented his status as one of Canada's most inspiring coaches. He took the helm of the Canadian national team at the 2002 Winter Olympics in Salt Lake City, Utah, where he had a team of NHL stars. Although expectations were high, Quinn's coaching brought them together. Team Canada faced their arch-rivals in the gold medal game, Team USA. The game was a tightly contested battle that went into overtime. It was there that Pat Quinn's coaching brilliance shone. He made a last-minute decision to send in a line change, and in a matter of seconds, Canada's Jarome Iginla set up a goal for Joe Sakic.

Canada won the gold, and Pat Quinn's coaching prowess became part of hockey history. Quinn's impact extended beyond the ice. He was a father figure to many of his players, offering guidance and support on and off the rink. His coaching philosophy was simple yet powerful: instill a love for the game, encourage teamwork, and teach life lessons far beyond hockey. Pat Quinn's coaching journey inspires all young Canadians who dream of becoming coaches or players. He demonstrated that anyone can significantly impact hockey with hard work, dedication, and a deep love for the game. Quinn's legacy lives on, not just in the trophies he won or the games he coached but in the lives he touched. He was more than just a coach; he was a mentor, a leader, and a symbol of Canadian hockey's heart and soul.

Like those of countless other inspiring coaches across Canada, his story serves as a testament to the power of guidance, mentorship, and the enduring love of a sport that has captured the hearts of a nation. These coaches, the unsung heroes behind the scenes, continue to shape the future of Canadian hockey, one player at a time.

Pat Quinn

BEHIND-THE-SCENES HEROES : NHL'S FIRST FULL-TIME BLACK OFFICIAL

Jay Sharrers is a pioneer in professional hockey officiating, having broken numerous barriers and made a significant impact. He became the National Hockey League's first full-time black official. This remarkable achievement speaks to his unwavering dedication, passion for the game, and the importance of diversity in sports.

Jay Sharrers was born in Alberta, Canada, in 1966, and from a young age, he developed a deep love for hockey. Like many Canadian children, he spent countless hours perfecting his skating and puck-handling skills on frozen ponds and rinks. Over time, he developed a unique perspective on the sport and an appreciation for its intricacies, which fueled his desire to become an official.

Jay Sharrers' journey as a hockey official was not without its challenges. In a sport where officials traditionally wore stripes, the sight of a young black man in the role was uncommon. This made his path to professional officiating even more unique. Despite adversity, he began his career working in the Western Hockey League (WHL) and the American Hockey League (AHL), where his commitment and knowledge of the game quickly set him apart. In 1990, Jay Sharrers achieved his dream when he was invited to officiate NHL games. He was the first full-time black official in the history of the NHL, breaking a significant racial barrier.

Sharrer's presence on the ice was commanding, and his knowledge of the rules and passion for the game was evident in every game he officiated. He officiated over 1,400 NHL games, including regular-season and playoff matchups. Jay Sharrers' legacy is one of inspiration and inclusivity. He inspired aspiring officials of all backgrounds to pursue their dreams and break through barriers. Sharrers showed that the love of hockey knows no bounds and that the ice is a place for anyone passionate about the sport. Even after retiring as an NHL official, Sharrers advocated for inclusivity and diversity in hockey, working with various organizations to promote these values.

Jay Sharrers' story is a testament to the fact that anything is possible if we set our minds to it and never give up on our dreams. If you are passionate about hockey and dream of becoming an official, follow in Sharrers' footsteps and pursue your dream with determination and resilience. Your love for the game can open doors to new opportunities and make history. Diversity strengthens the sport of hockey, and your unique perspective can be an asset to the game you love.

Jay Sharrers

THE UNSUNG HERO: SUPPORT STAFF

Joey Moss was an admired and beloved figure in hockey who demonstrated how support staff can profoundly impact the sport. Born in 1963 with Down syndrome, Joey faced several challenges from a young age, including peer bullying and difficulties within the education system. Nevertheless, Joey's love for hockey remained strong, and he was determined to overcome these obstacles.

Even as a young boy, Joey's passion for hockey was evident. He spent countless hours watching the game on TV and studying the play of his favorite players. He often attended games in person, cheering on his cherished Edmonton Oilers.

In the early 1980s, Wayne Gretzky discovered Joey working at a local cleaning service. Gretzky was deeply impressed by Joey's infectious enthusiasm for the game and his remarkable memory for hockey statistics. Recognizing his potential, Gretzky offered Joey a part-time job as a locker room attendant for the Oilers.

Joey quickly became an indispensable part of the team, assisting players in getting dressed and organizing equipment. However, his impact surpassed these duties. Joey became the Oilers' unofficial dressing room DJ, and his song choices became vital to the team's pre-game rituals, motivating and inspiring the players.

Moreover, Joey's spirit and positivity infused the Oilers' locker room, endearing him to players, coaches, and staff alike. The camaraderie and unity that Joey helped foster significantly contributed to the Oilers' success during the 1980s.

Joey Moss became an iconic and beloved figure in Edmonton, inspiring many with his determination, enthusiasm, and devotion to the game. He advocated for inclusivity and acceptance, raising awareness of Down syndrome and supporting individuals with disabilities in reaching their full potential.

Joey Moss passed away tragically in October 2020, but his legacy lives on. His story continues to inspire people of all ages and backgrounds, exemplifying the profound impact that support staff can have in sports. Joey Moss was not just an unsung hero of the Edmonton Oilers but an unsung hero of the hockey world.

Joey's legacy is a reminder that everyone has something meaningful to contribute, regardless of their circumstances. He taught us that dreams can be achieved when we set our minds to them and never give up. Joey Moss remains an enduring source of inspiration, and his memory will forever be cherished.

Joey Moss

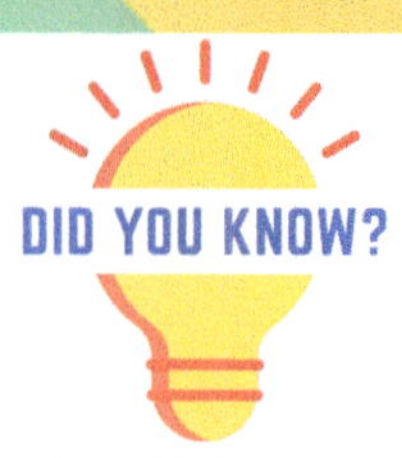

Topic	Fact/Trivia
Inspiring Coaches	
Scotty Bowman's Record	Scotty Bowman holds the record for the most Stanley Cup championships won by a head coach, with nine titles.
Coaching Legend	Toe Blake, who coached the Montreal Canadiens, won an incredible eight Stanley Cup championships as a head coach.
Pat Burns' Journey	Pat Burns, a former police officer, won the Jack Adams Award three times and led the New Jersey Devils to a Stanley Cup victory in 2003.
Behind-the-Scenes Heroes: Officials	
First Female Official	In 2019, Katie Guay became the first woman to officiate an NHL preseason game, breaking gender barriers in the sport.
Kerry Fraser's Iconic Hair	Long-time NHL referee Kerry Fraser was known for his distinctive flowing hair and officiated over 1,900 NHL games.
Don Koharski and the "Donut Incident"	Referee Don Koharski became famous for an incident when coach Jim Schoenfeld shouted, "Have another donut!" during a game.
How Support Staff Contribute to the Sport	
Joey Moss' Legacy	Joey Moss, a locker room attendant with Down syndrome, left a lasting legacy with the Edmonton Oilers, becoming an iconic figure in the sport.
Equipment Managers	Equipment managers play a critical role in ensuring players have properly fitted gear and maintaining equipment throughout the season.
Athletic Trainers	Athletic trainers are responsible for player health and well-being, tending to injuries, and ensuring their fitness throughout the season.

10. MOST EXCITING MATCHES

- 1972 Summit Series: Canada vs. the Soviet Union
- Mario's Miracle: The 1987 Canada Cup Showdown
- The Golden Moment: 2010 Winter Olympics
- 2014 Sochi Olympics Men's Hockey Final
- 2016 World Cup of Hockey Final: Canada vs. Team Europe
- 2020 IIHF World Junior Championship Final: Canada vs. Russia

1972 SUMMIT SERIES: CANADA VS. THE SOVIET UNION

Welcome, young hockey enthusiasts and aspiring players of Canada! I am excited to take you on an exhilarating journey back in time to one of the most iconic moments in hockey history: the 1972 Summit Series between Canada and the Soviet Union. This tournament was more than just a game; it was a test of sportsmanship, a battle of wills, and a clash of styles during the height of the Cold War.

Let's set the scene: in 1972, when the world was divided, tensions between the East and the West were high. The hockey world was no exception, with Canada and the Soviet Union each boasting formidable teams.

In Canada, the nation was brimming with hope and expectation, eagerly awaiting the arrival of the Soviet squad, a team that was often shrouded in mystery. The Soviets had a unique style of play, emphasizing team coordination and using a mesmerizing "cycle" offense where the puck moved with unparalleled precision.

The series began with Team Canada facing a cold reality. The Soviet Union dominated the first four games, shocking our Canadian team. But as the losses piled up, a fierce determination began to take hold. The young and seasoned players of Canada, including heroes like Paul Henderson, Phil Esposito, Yvan Cournoyer, Bobby Clarke, and Ken Dryden, came together, united by a common purpose: to show the world the true spirit of Canadian hockey. In game five, in front of a home crowd in Canada, our heroes made a resounding comeback. The roar of the fans echoed throughout the nation, propelling the team to victory.

The atmosphere was electric, as Canada's young stars inspired a nation.

The series raged on, with both teams trading wins. Every game felt like a battle of titans as the world watched with bated breath. Canada's grit and the Soviets' skill collided on the ice, creating moments that still give us chills today.

But in the eighth and final game in Moscow, the Summit Series reached its breathtaking conclusion. The tension was palpable as the game was tied 5-5 with just over a minute left.

Then, in a forever-etched moment in hockey history, Paul Henderson scored the series-clinching goal. Team Canada emerged victorious, and the celebrations across the country were legendary.

The Summit Series wasn't just about winning a tournament; it was a statement to the world. It showed the unifying power of sport and how hockey could transcend politics and borders to unite people. It taught us that no matter the challenges, the passion and heart of Canadian hockey players would always shine through.

Most importantly, the Summit Series showed us that dreams can come true. Even when faced with overwhelming odds, the Canadian team never gave up. They fought until the very end, and they achieved something truly remarkable.

So, young players, remember this story when you step onto the ice. The 1972 Summit Series is more than a historic event; it's a symbol of what can be achieved through determination, teamwork, and the unwavering spirit of the Canadian game.

It's a reminder that every time you lace up your skates, you're part of a legacy that stretches back to those incredible days.

One day, you'll create your unforgettable moments in hockey, just like those heroes did in 1972.

MARIO'S MIRACLE: THE 1987 CANADA CUP SHOWDOWN

In the late 1980s, the world witnessed an unforgettable moment in Canadian hockey history - the 1987 Canada Cup Final. This tournament brought together the best elite talents from both sides of the border for a thrilling showdown. However, it was the final game, a clash of hockey titans between Canada and the Soviet Union, that sent shockwaves through the hockey world.

Let's travel back in time to the moment and relive the excitement. The 1987 Canada Cup was a battleground for hockey superstars. Team Canada, with legendary players like Wayne Gretzky, Mark Messier, Paul Coffey, and many others.

They faced off against the Soviet Union's equally talented squad, including the likes of Igor Larionov, Viacheslav Fetisov, and Sergei Makarov. Throughout the tournament, both teams displayed incredible skills, demonstrating why they were considered the best in the world. As the series progressed, excitement and tension grew, leading to a showdown that would go down in history.

The final game occurred in Hamilton, Ontario, with the Canadian fans passionately rallying behind their heroes. Every shot, pass, and save was executed with precision, displaying the artistry of the sport. The game was an intense battle from start to finish.

The most remarkable moment came in the third overtime period, an exhausting and thrilling affair. With just a few seconds remaining, the unthinkable occurred. Mario Lemieux, a rising star who would become a legend, scored the game-winning goal. The arena erupted in pandemonium as Canada clinched the title.

The 1987 Canada Cup was more than just a hockey tournament; it was a testament to Canadian hockey players' dedication, skill, and heart. It reminded us of the enduring spirit of the game and the indomitable will of those who wear the maple leaf on their chest. This story teaches us that dreams can come true when you combine unwavering dedication with raw talent.

It shows us that teamwork and passion can propel you to victory, even when faced with the toughest competition. It's a symbol of the unifying power of hockey, how the sport can bring a nation together in celebration.

So, every time young hockey enthusiasts step onto the ice, they should remember this tale. Let it be a source of inspiration and a testament to what can be achieved when aiming for greatness. After all, the 1987 Canada Cup Final was not just a tournament but a legendary moment in Canadian hockey that continues to inspire generations of players.

Mario Lemieux- Hall of Fame

THE GOLDEN MOMENT: 2010 WINTER OLYMPICS

Let's take a trip down memory lane to a moment that still sends shivers down the spine of every true hockey fan - the 2010 Winter Olympics in Vancouver, Canada. It was a gold medal game for the ages, where our beloved Team Canada faced off against their rivals from the United States.

It was more than just a game; it was a battle for national pride, a showdown of two hockey powerhouses, and a chance to etch one's name into the annals of Canadian sports history. The year was 2010, and the world had its eyes fixed on Vancouver, where the Olympics were in full swing. For every young hockey player, this was a dream come true.

The best of the best from around the globe had gathered, and Canada, as the host nation, had its eyes firmly set on the coveted gold medal. It was extraordinary because these were the first Olympic Games held in Canada since 1988, making the tournament even more significant.

Our heroes were a star-studded lineup with names like Sidney Crosby, Jonathan Toews, and Roberto Luongo. The arena was a sea of red and white, with fans cheering for Team Canada. The tension was palpable as they faced their arch-rivals, the United States, in the gold medal game.

The Americans were no pushovers. They were determined, skillful, and hungry for victory. The game was a roller-coaster, with both teams trading blows and showing off their incredible skills.

Jonathan Toews scored two magnificent goals in the first period, showcasing his leadership and skill. Roberto Luongo made 34 saves in the game, standing tall between the pipes.

And Jarome Iginla's perfect pass set up the iconic moment. The third period ended with a 2-2 tie, and overtime was upon us—the hearts of a nation beat as one as Canada pressed forward relentlessly. And then, in an instant that would go down in history, it happened.

Sidney Crosby, our captain and a young superstar, received a pass from Jarome Iginla and calmly buried the puck in the back of the net. The entire nation erupted in joy, celebrating Sidney Crosby's golden goal. The 2010 Winter Olympics gold medal became Canadian history's most-watched hockey game.

The 2010 Winter Olympics were more than just a hockey tournament; they were a testament to the spirit of Canadian hockey. It showed the world the power of determination, teamwork, and passion. It proved that no challenge is too great when you believe in your abilities and work together.

As young players, this story should inspire you. It should remind you that dreams can come true on the biggest stages. It should show you that no matter how young or inexperienced you may be, you can achieve greatness with dedication and a love for the game.

The 2010 Winter Olympics weren't just a sporting event but a symbol of Canadian pride and the unifying power of hockey. And for every young Canadian with a hockey dream, they are a testament to what can be achieved when you dare to chase those dreams.

2014 SOCHI OLYMPICS MEN'S HOCKEY FINAL

The 2014 Winter Olympics in Sochi, Russia, saw a thrilling showdown on the ice between Canadian and Swedish hockey players. This piece will revisit the incredible moment when Team Canada showed sheer dominance. Young Canadian hockey enthusiasts and budding players can learn from this historic event.

The Sochi Olympics was a global spectacle, and Canada was eager to prove that hockey was more than just a sport but a way of life. The Canadian team boasted extraordinary talent, including Sidney Crosby, Jonathan Toews, and Shea Weber. The gold medal game was a rematch of the 1994 game, with Sweden looking to avenge their loss from two decades prior. Canada was the defending Olympic gold medalist, and the pressure to retain their title was immense.

The game was set, and the atmosphere was electric as the puck dropped. Canadian fans, dressed in red and white, were passionately rallying behind their team. Canada dominated initially, showcasing their incredible talent and unwavering determination. Jonathan Toews opened the scoring in the first period, providing an early lead and setting the tone for the game. Sidney Crosby added another goal in the second period, extending the lead to 2-0. Canada's captain led by example and reminded the world why he was one of the best in the game.

Canada's grip on the game tightened as the clock wound down, with their relentless defense and precision passing leaving Sweden struggling to find an answer. The defensive plays led by Shea Weber and the brilliant saves by goaltender Roberto Luongo were spectacular.

Canada's teamwork and individual brilliance blended seamlessly. In the final period, Chris Kunitz secured Canada's second consecutive Olympic gold medal with his goal. It was a moment of pure joy and celebration as the nation watched in awe, knowing their team was the best in the world.

The 2014 Sochi Olympics gold medal game symbolized Canadian excellence in hockey. It was a reminder of the values that underpin the sport: hard work, dedication, and teamwork. It showed the world that Canadians play with a sense of purpose and a love for the game that knows no bounds.

As young players, you can learn from this story. It serves as a reminder that greatness is within reach if you work together and believe in your abilities. It shows that hockey is not just a sport but a way of life in Canada, a source of pride, and a symbol of what can be achieved through unwavering dedication.

The 2014 Sochi Olympics gold medal game was a testament to the enduring spirit of Canadian hockey. It was a moment that inspired a nation and continues to inspire generations of young players who dream of stepping onto the world stage one day.

By Atos - Atos at the Olympic Winter Games Ice Hockey - Was it really a score or not- Russia againts Slovenia - score 4-2Uploaded by Sporti, CC BY-SA 2.0, https://commons.wikimedia.org/w/index.php?curid=31161555

2016 WORLD CUP OF HOCKEY FINAL: CANADA VS. TEAM EUROPE

In hockey, some Canadian stories go beyond the ordinary, and the 2016 World Cup of Hockey Final between Canada and Team Europe is one such tale. The championship held all the drama and excitement as Team Canada faced an unexpected adversary in Team Europe.

Imagine yourself in 2016, when the hockey world had its eyes on Toronto, Canada. The World Cup of Hockey had returned, and the stakes were higher than ever. The best teams from around the globe had gathered to compete in a thrilling tournament, with one showdown that would leave an indelible mark on Canadian hockey history.

Team Canada was the favorite, boasting some of the world's most incredible talent, including Sidney Crosby, Jonathan Toews, and Carey Price, making them a force to be reckoned with. Their opponent, however, was something of a surprise. Team Europe was a unique collection of European talent featuring players from countries not typically seen as a single team in international competitions. It was the first time Team Europe had competed in an international tournament, adding an extra layer of excitement to the championship.

As the final game dawned, the atmosphere in the arena was electric. Fans of all ages were on the edge of their seats, ready to watch their heroes in action. The game began, and the two teams clashed in a contest that was nothing short of extraordinary.

For Team Canada, it was a match that tested their skills and determination. Team Europe was relentless, putting up an intense fight, and the game remained scoreless for much of the first period. But young Jonathan Toews, a name synonymous with clutch performances, opened the scoring in the second period with a spectacular goal, providing an early lead and setting the tone for the game.

But Team Europe was about to keep going. They fought back and tied the game at 1-1, setting the stage for a nail-biting finish. As the clock ticked, the world watched in anticipation, and the atmosphere was electric.

And then, in a moment that sent the crowd into a frenzy, Brad Marchand scored the game-winning goal in overtime. The arena erupted with cheers and celebrations as Canada clinched the championship. It was a hard-fought victory, a testament to the skill and tenacity of Team Canada, and it showed the world that no matter the odds, Canadians could always rise to the occasion.

The 2016 World Cup of Hockey Final was more than just a game; it was a reminder of the greatness that hockey represents for Canada. It showcased the values of teamwork, dedication, and perseverance that are the essence of the sport. This moment continues to inspire young players across the nation.

So, remember this story, young hockey enthusiasts, as you lace up your skates and take to the ice. It's a testament to what can be achieved through hard work, unity, and an unwavering belief in your abilities.

It's a reminder that in the world of hockey, as in life, every challenge is an opportunity to shine.

The 2016 World Cup of Hockey Final between Canada and Team Europe is a story you can carry with you as you step onto the rink, reminding you that greatness is within reach, no matter who the opponent may be.

2020 IIHF WORLD JUNIOR CHAMPIONSHIP FINAL: CANADA VS. RUSSIA

In hockey, some stories define the sport's essence and inspire generations of players. The 2020 IIHF World Junior Championship Final between Canada and Russia is one of those stories. It was a gold medal game that unfolded with all the drama and intensity you can imagine, showcasing the heart-pounding excitement of hockey at its finest.

Imagine yourself transported to the year 2020 when the hockey world's attention was fixed on the IIHF World Junior Championship.

For Canada, this tournament was a competition and a chance to prove their hockey prowess to the world, a tradition that runs deep in the nation's veins.

This story is even more special because the 2020 IIHF World Junior Championship was the final tournament to be played before the COVID-19 pandemic. It was a moment of triumph and celebration before the world changed, a reminder of how hockey can bring joy and unity even in the most challenging times.

As the tournament progressed, Canada faced their long-time rivals, Russia, in the gold medal game. It was a matchup that ignited the passion of fans, young and old, a classic showdown between two hockey giants.

The atmosphere in the arena was electric. Canadian supporters donned red and white jerseys, passionately rallying behind the young stars who represented their nation. Russia, with its rich hockey history, was determined to claim victory. The stage was set for a battle that would be etched in the annals of hockey history.
The game that followed was nothing short of extraordinary. It was a tightly contested match where every pass, shot, and save mattered. The players on both sides displayed their incredible skills and unwavering determination.

Canada's team was packed with young talent, future NHL stars in the making. Connor McMichael, who scored two goals in the Final game, and Alexis Lafrenière, named the tournament MVP, were just a few of the many players who shone brightly that day. As the game progressed, it became evident that victory was within reach, but the Russian team fought back with equal vigor.

The goals went back and forth, with each team refusing to give an inch. The crowd was on the edge of their seats, their hearts pounding as the seconds ticked.

Ultimately, Canada emerged victorious with a 4-3 scoreline, securing yet another World Junior Championship title. The arena erupted in cheers, and the national celebrations were legendary. It was a testament to Canadian hockey players' unwavering spirit and dedication.

Here's another remarkable fact: the 2020 IIHF World Junior Championship Final was the most-watched hockey game in Canadian history since the 2010 Olympic gold medal. It is a testament to the sport's popularity and the game's significance.

The 2020 IIHF World Junior Championship Final was more than just a game; it symbolized the passion and heart that Canadians pour into the sport. It reminded young players that dreams can be realized with hard work, dedication, and a deep love for the game.

So, remember this story, young hockey enthusiasts, as you hit the ice with your sticks and skates. Let it be a beacon of inspiration, a reminder that every time you play, you're part of a legacy and the great tradition of Canadian hockey.

The 2020 IIHF World Junior Championship Final was a thrilling tale that continues to inspire young players to reach for the stars, just as the heroes on that day did in their quest for victory.

DID YOU KNOW?

Fact/Trivia	Description
"The Miracle on Ice" Defeat	Canada's defeat to the United States in the 1980 Winter Olympics, a historic upset.
The 1972 Summit Series	Canada's victory over the Soviet Union in the historic 1972 Summit Series.
The "Golden Goal"	Sidney Crosby's 2010 Winter Olympics game-winning goal against the United States.
Team Canada's Triple Gold Club Members	Only seven players in hockey history have achieved the Triple Gold Club.
Dominance in World Junior Championships	Canada's strong performance in the IIHF World Junior Championships.
The Canada Cup Dynasty	Canada's dominance in the Canada Cup international tournament in the late 1970s-80s.
Most Stanley Cup Wins	Canadian NHL teams have collectively won the most Stanley Cups in the league's history.
Birth of the NHL	The NHL, the premier professional hockey league, was founded in Montreal, Canada, in 1917.
The Paul Henderson Goal	Paul Henderson's game-winning goal in the 1972 Summit Series for Canada.
The Great One	Wayne Gretzky, considered the greatest hockey player of all time, is a Canadian legend.

11. QUIZ TIME
Fun Corner!

Quiz Time

1. Which Canadian hockey player scored the game-winning goal in the 1972 Summit Series?

(A) Wayne Gretzky (B) Bobby Orr (C) Paul Henderson
(D) Mario Lemieux

2. Who is the only Canadian hockey player to have won the Stanley Cup, the Olympic gold medal, and the World Championship gold medal more than once?

(A) Sidney Crosby (B) Connor McDavid (C) Ken Dryden (D) Darryl Sittler

3. What do we call the area where ice hockey is played?

(A) An ice mark (B) An ice rink (C) An ice course (D) An ice field

4. How many players can each team simultaneously have on the ice rink?

(A) 11 (B) 8 (C) 6 (D) None

Quiz Time

5. In which city is the headquarters of the International Ice Hockey Federation based?

(A) New York (B) Zurich (C) Helsinki (D) Montreal

6. Puck is made out of which material?

(A) Steel (B) Wood (C) Plastic (D) Rubber

7. In ice hockey, which team starts with possessing the puck?

(A) The away team (B) The home team (C) The team winning the puck drop (D) None

8. The space between the leg pads of a goalie is called ....

(A) A double-hole (B) A four-hole (C) A six-hole (D) A five-hole

Quiz Time

9. The Big Six, a group of 6 national teams that dominated men's international ice hockey, consists of the United States, Canada, Finland, Sweden, ..., and the ....

(A)Poland and Germany (B) Russia and the Czech Republic
(C) Norway and Belarus (D) None

10. Minor the penalty in ice hockey last for how many minutes?

 (A)2 minutes (B) 3 minutes (C) 4 minutes (D) 5 minutes

11. Ice hockey is the official national winter sport of which country?

(A)Russia (B) Norway (C)Canada (D) USA

12. The winning team of the NHL Finals is given which trophy?

(A) The Memorial Cup (B) The Super Bowl (C)The Stanley Cup (D) None

Quiz Time

13. Who won the IIHF World Championship in 2022?

(A) Canada (B)Russia (C)Norway (D)Finland

14. The National Hockey League or NHL is a professional hockey league in which two countries?

(A) Canada & Russia (B)Russia & Finland (C)Norway & Finland (D)Canada & USA

15. Who won the IIHF World Championship?

(A) Canada (B)Russia (C)Norway (D)Finland.

16. Who won the 2023 IIHF Women's World Championship?

(A) Canada (B)USA (C)Norway (D)Finland.

17. Which 2 countries replaced Russia and Belarus in 2023 Men's Ice Hockey World Championships

(A) Canada & USA (B)France and Austria (C)Norway& Finland (D)None

Quiz Time-Answer

1. (C) Paul Henderson
2. (A) Sidney Crosby
3. (B) An ice rink
4. (C) 6
5. (B) Zurich
6. (D) Rubber
7. (C) The team winning the puck drop
8. (D) A five-hole
9. (B) Russia and the Czech Republic
10. (A) 2 minutes
11. (C) Canada
12. (C) The Stanley Cup
13. (D) Finland
14. (D) Canada & USA
15. (A) Canada
16. (B) USA
17. (B) France and Austria

Please let us know how we're doing by leaving us a review.

CONCLUSION

As we end "The Most Inspiring Hockey Stories of All Time for Young Canadians," it's important to remember that hockey is more than just a sport; it's a way of life for Canadians. From the legendary players who graced the ice with their extraordinary skills to the kids who aspire to be the next Wayne Gretzky, this book has taken you on a journey through the heart of the rink.

Hockey encompasses more than just goals and assists; it's about the values and traditions that unite us. It's about sportsmanship and teamwork, the coaches and mentors shaping the players on and off the ice. It's about the women who have broken barriers and the resilient individuals who triumph in adversity. As we've explored historic Stanley Cup moments, celebrated rookie sensations, and delved into the spirit of the game, we've discovered that the magic of hockey lies in its ability to capture hearts and inspire dreams. It transcends generations, connecting Canadians of all ages. Relive unforgettable matches, from the 1972 Summit Series to the 2016 World Cup of Hockey Final. These games embody the passion and the pursuit of excellence. Our book introduces heroes on and off the ice, support staff, and young talents who carry the dreams of a nation. Every frozen pond and backyard rink is a place of endless possibilities.

Hockey reflects the Canadian spirit, teaching us to work hard, never give up, and play as a team. It's a story of resilience, passion, and dreams.

These chapters hold tales of life, unity, and inspiration. Whether a young player or fan, let these stories remind you of greatness within the game and yourself. Step onto the rink, as you are the future of Canadian hockey, and your journey has just begun. Play hard, dream big, and keep the spirit of hockey alive.

Thank you once again.

Dr. Fanatomy